DEDICATION

- My firstborn Meliah, for editing it and cheering me on

- My younger three children—Makenzie, Carson & Ryder—for helping me understand how much God loves me

- The parents who may see themselves in these stories, including my own

- My patients, for the incredible gift of their trust

- My husband, for always believing that I can do anything

- And most of all God, for His unbelievable patience and unexpected sense of humor

CONTENTS

PROLOGUE

I have loved writing for as long as I can remember, and yet I never planned to write this book—or even thought about it—until God had His way. I am still amused now when I think back to the moment that I realized I had started a book at my Heavenly Father's prompting *months earlier* without even knowing it. There had been the occasional social media post about God's leading in my life and the friends who told me that I should turn them into a book. Then, there had been my primary care physician and her oft-repeated suggestion that I should write a book about the almost comical number of rare and difficult-to-diagnose diseases that have plagued my family—though she herself hates to write and has never known that I don't. (And that, my friends, is a story for another day.)

My soul has been drawn to writing since the days when it could only be done with pen and paper. And God had given me a gift even then that it would take me decades to realize was mine and finally use for Him. Until now, I had forgotten all about the statewide writing contest I entered in early elementary school that won my family a trip on a seemingly magical train at Christmastime in Massachusetts. But I could never forget the many diaries that I have kept since I was able to read and write—the earliest of which my daughters have had a good laugh at because maturity and writing skill are two entirely different things. Some of the diaries, I am still not

1

ready to reopen, because they would take me back to a time too painful to revisit (such as the years surrounding my daughter Makenzie's bone marrow transplant).

Yet in every case, writing has been so therapeutic for me. Some people self-medicate with alcohol or drugs. Others soothe their souls with relationships or shopping sprees. As for me, writing is my medicine. And through His Holy Spirit, God has made me understand that this gift, too, was always meant to be used to heal others for Him—just as the M.D. after my name has been.

Before God could use me to share His love with others, however, He had to show me how much He loves me first—and show me He has. I was born into a Christian family, but it wasn't until I was an adult that I truly understood how fortunate I was to have been taught about my Savior from the very beginning. A third generation Seventh-day Adventist on my father's side and a fifth generation Seventh-day Adventist on my mother's, I have never known what life without the Bible and an understanding of *The Great Controversy*[1] between God and Satan would be like. But as every adult who was raised in a Christian home can attest to, it's not enough to simply grow up in church and hear the name of Jesus for eighteen years. I had to experience Him for myself—and not only in the good times.

I could never prove through earthly means that it was actually God—or one of His angels—who acted in these moments when I needed Him most, and that's okay. I recognized my amazing Friend when He showed up for me, just as Jesus said would be the case. "My sheep hear my voice, and I know them, and they follow Me" (John 10:27 New King James Version). Many of these personal "God moments" happened years ago and are not the subject of this particular book, yet they have had a lasting influence and are certainly one of the reasons I was able to see God within the stories that I did include. So, it only seems fitting that I share *one* of these experiences with you—especially considering that if not for God's intervention on this specific occasion, this book would not exist.

About this day, I have never told anyone until now. Some of the details have naturally faded from my memory during the years that have elapsed, but the important ones remain. I was enjoying a pool party in the summer months of Massachusetts as a guest at someone's home. Many of my schoolmates from Edgewood Elementary School were there, including my older sister, Heidi. I cannot remember if my younger brother Heath was with us, but I do know that my mother was watching from the pool deck with many of the other parents she knew from church. I couldn't have been more than eight or nine years old because my youngest brother Hyatt didn't exist, and I hadn't learned how to swim yet.

Little girls who cannot swim are supposed to stay in the shallow end of the pool—and, of course, that had been my good intention. But as children often do, I inched closer and closer to the deep end without realizing it. The image of the exact area of the pool where danger met me is still etched into my brain decades later. My feet could no longer feel the bottom of the pool, and the water was high enough that it began to engulf my face. I had been hugging the wall of the pool on my journey toward deeper waters, but like the floor a moment earlier, the pool's wall was suddenly out of my reach. I searched for the floor with my feet as best I could—and when I didn't find it, panic took over.

Within the invisible box of water that now surrounded me completely, I am certain that I kicked and screamed and wondered if I was going to die—until I felt the arms that lifted me up and set my feet back on the pool floor that they had wandered from. Immediately, my heart was filled with two competing emotions—utter relief and immense embarrassment. Naturally, I assumed that someone at the pool party had seen me drowning and come to my rescue. How *couldn't* there have been with all of the ruckus

I (thought that I) had made? I was prepared to thank them—once I knew who had actually saved me—and then hide my face and try to live down my new reputation as the kid who had been flailing around and shrieking in the pool because she couldn't swim.

But when I looked up, **no one was there**. No hero or de facto lifeguard. No onlooking classmates or church members. Not even my overprotective mother (whom I immediately decided it was best *not* to share my near drowning experience with). It was at that moment that it occurred to me that God had sent an angel to rescue me. No other explanation made sense. And yet I didn't understand how I had come so close to drowning without anyone noticing.

So as human nature often does when it comes to God's interventions, I began to doubt my experience. *I must have saved myself.* This is what I told myself each time the unforgettable memories of that day resurfaced. *I must have found my way back to the shallow end of the pool on my own.* For this reason, I didn't share the story with anyone else. How could I when I didn't even fully understand it myself?

Decades later, I found myself searching for answers. It didn't take long to find them: multiple cautionary, real-life stories and surveillance videos documenting the drownings and near-drownings of children in public pools filled with other swimmers, countless websites explaining that drowning is *often* a silent (and quick) process, and numerous, unrelated swim safety campaigns that all used the same rhyming, new-to-me phrase to teach parents that kids "can drown without a sound." The videos were especially shocking—and difficult to watch. Even in hindsight, the drownings wouldn't have been recognizable if not for the editing that added brightly colored arrows and circles to alert viewers to the distressed swimmer's location in the pool. It's hard to describe the emotions I felt as

I watched children struggle silently under circumstances that were eerily similar to the ones that almost took my life.

Finally, I understood my experience in its true light. And I knew that an angel *must* have been there to intervene—just as I had known it that day in the pool years ago before I allowed my human skepticism to muddy the waters for me. I could never insinuate that my young life was more valuable than the lives of the children who were lost during their own unnoticed drownings—for undoubtedly, it wasn't. But I do believe that God had a work for me to do (and that writing this book was one of them).

These forty lessons from God were written over a two-year period that began in April of 2020. A few of these lessons tell stories that happened years earlier, but most of them occurred as I was writing the book itself. I didn't know that there would be forty chapters when God first gave me the idea for this book. I simply wrote as the experiences and insights came, never knowing when the next one would present itself. Sometimes there were two in one week—and because I'm working full time, I would have to jot the titles down so that I wouldn't forget the stories while I was waiting to find time to write. Other times, a month would pass without anything noteworthy occurring at all. I never knew when the next story would arrive—I left that in God's hands. And to be honest, it felt kind of exciting. But I always recognized each new story—and the spiritual lessons it taught—when it did eventually come, and I would be a fool to think that it was anything other than the Holy Spirit who opened my eyes to its significance.

This book is God's well-orchestrated design, and I still cannot believe that He used *me* to write it. If you find anything good within its pages, then share it with someone else who may need the comfort and hope that only Heaven can truly provide. And if you see me face-to-face and want to say something positive about this book, don't tell me that I'm a good writer. Praise God with me instead, and tell me that you feel more loved by the Father and Son than you did before.

ABBA KNOWS BEST

"Trust in the Lord with all your heart, and lean not on your own understanding; in all your ways acknowledge Him, and He shall direct your paths." Proverbs 3:5-6 NKJV

God's plans are always smarter than mine, and when I ask Him to block my plans if He can see something important that I cannot, He literally (and graciously) saves me from myself. After each disappointment and "no" for an answer, I can clearly see the reason why in due time. The evidences of His personalized, deliberate, and wise interventions on my behalf are all around me. God is real folks, and prayer actually changes things (over and over again) in ways that would be very unlikely to occur randomly. I just can't make this stuff up, and I am feeling grateful and so very loved.

"And now for the rest of the story," as the late Paul Harvey always said.[1] It's God's story mostly, and a little bit of mine. You ask me how I know He is real? There are too many reasons to list at one time. For now, I will just say that unlikely things have been brought to pass as a result of my prayer life—things that worldly odds wouldn't be able to explain convincingly when taken as a group. *No one* is this lucky on their own.

God can and does say no to my prayer requests at times, but when He does—and things don't turn out like I had asked or imagined—I can easily see (eventually) why His way was so much better than the one I had planned. Sometimes—as in this very case—I shudder to think of what would have happened if God hadn't answered no, and I had gotten my own way. There are moments when I need to thank Him specifically for saving me from myself because I couldn't see the future as He did.

When I was given my current job (another answer to prayer), Jason and I assumed that we would live in Hagerstown, where I now work. We were hopeful that our beloved home would sell quickly in the hot Nashville housing market, and we could buy a new house in Maryland without having to rent temporarily. Our Maryland realtor, Dee, took us to ten houses in the two days that we visited, and we only liked two of them, so we began to realize that it would be more difficult to find a house than we had thought. The first one went under contract quickly, and the second one—the only remaining house that we wanted—was about to go under contract, too. Our realtor asked us if we wanted to make an offer with a house-to-sell contingency because the realtor for the sellers had actually been on the other side of a similar contract with our realtor previously. It had worked out well for *them* in the end. As I thought about this prospect, I began to feel optimistic that it could also work for us.

A wise pastor friend, Ken Wetmore, had once told us that whenever he didn't know what do to in a certain situation and God wasn't making it obvious, he would simply use the brain that God had given him and do what seemed right in his own eyes. Then he would pray, "If You can see something I can't, God, and I'm not making the right decision, then please close the door and block this path." He said that the one time he bulldozed through with his plan anyways, even as road blocks appeared, he had surely regretted it for years. So, we did the same thing and made an offer on the house, while praying that God would close the door if He knew that it wasn't the best thing for us.

We had three weeks to get a contract on our Nashville home. I prayed boldly about it, but our house didn't sell. During this three-week period, a couple looked at our house and their realtor texted ours to say that the wife (who had looked at many other homes) "loves it—it's perfect for her. They're going to lay/pray about it." We liked the idea of a couple praying about our home. Surely God would tell them to buy our house. Some other couples liked our house, as well ("it's down to your house and just one other," we had heard a couple of times). But one potential buyer had family in another part of Nashville, and the other one wanted to renovate our master bathroom and didn't think that they'd be able to get it done before their new baby arrived just three weeks later. We figured that the couple who was going to "lay and pray" about it would take a week or so to sleep on it and either make an offer or not. And so, when we didn't hear back from them after a couple of weeks, we assumed that they had purchased another house instead. Eventually, we forgot about them.

Multiple times, couples asked to see our house on Sabbath. The choice we were given was to show the house on Saturday or not at all, because "no other day will work for them," their realtor would relay. Knowing that we were losing those potential buyers permanently—and that most of the couples who actually saw our house liked it—we still said no (although we always felt disappointed). Even our own realtor didn't understand why we had made this decision, as a previous Seventh-day Adventist couple she had represented had been willing to show their house on Saturdays. But Jason and I knew that God could and would sell our house in spite of the lost Saturday buyers—especially because we were honoring Him. How could we ask Him to help us sell our home and then show it on the very day that He had asked us to keep holy and not do any work? The third time this happened, I felt bolder and less discouraged, and I said out loud to Jason when we got the familiar (Saturday showing only) text, "*God wins.*"

The sellers of the home in Hagerstown offered to extend the three-week contract by another two weeks, and we went for it again. "Why not? Maybe God needs more time to sell our house," I (naively) thought. Of course, the reality is that God could've sold it in one *day*, if He'd actually wanted to. But that didn't happen. At the end of the five weeks when there was still no buyer, we let the contract expire and got our earnest money back.

Meanwhile, no jobs opened up for Jason at the Seventh-day Adventist school in Hagerstown, as we had hoped. I was more disappointed than he was. At first, I couldn't see God's reasoning at all because we had been praying about a job for him as faithfully as we had been praying about our house—and for the job that I had ultimately gotten. Suddenly, we didn't know which city Jason was even going to work in.

Weeks went by, and Jason unexpectedly found a new job posting for a 6th grade teaching position at the Seventh-day Adventist school in Columbia, which was an hour away from Hagerstown. This time of the year, most positions in the SDA schools had already been filled. (But this position opened up at the last minute when a faculty member decided to go to the mission field.) A couple of weeks and lots of prayers later, and the job was Jason's. We shuttered at the thought that we had nearly been trapped in a contract on a house that was an hour (plus traffic) away from Jason's job, and we knew that God had saved us from our ignorant plans.

What we *really* didn't expect was the events that followed. Just three days after Jason and I knew that we would need to buy a house that was located between the towns of Hagerstown and Columbia instead, we got a call from our Nashville realtor. An offer on our house was finally coming.

I naturally assumed that the offer had been made by the couple who had seen our house most recently and liked it enough that they had asked to see the HOA documents. But I was wrong. The offer was coming from the "laying/praying" couple from **ten weeks** earlier. It was now clear that God had somehow caused them to delay their offer until the very week when Jason and I knew where he would be working. Had they made an offer even a couple of weeks earlier, we would probably have found another house in Hagerstown and gotten ourselves stuck in a contract on a home in the wrong city (again)—only this time we wouldn't have been able to get out of it (because we would've had a contract on our Nashville home, so no contingency could expire). Then Jason wouldn't have been able to apply for the job in Columbia (which was the perfect first job for him, by the way).

And so, this ends my latest "God story." God is alive and continually works in my life—sometimes to woo me with His love and blessings, and other times to help me learn to trust Him better and protect me with the answer "no" when I can't see the danger right in front of me. I have come to trust Him far more by going through the uncomfortable waiting periods than I could have ever learned to trust Him through the good times. I have learned that I would rather struggle through something and know that He's in charge of the final outcome than find things easy and know that I'm the one in charge. I have also discovered that the more I share the incredible things that He has done for me, the more remarkable things He does.

CHAPTER TWO

BRILLIANT WITH DEMENTIA

"THE FEAR OF THE LORD IS THE BEGINNING OF WISDOM, AND KNOWLEDGE OF THE HOLY ONE IS UNDERSTANDING." PROVERBS 9:10 NIV

I t was the beginning of the COVID-19 pandemic, and I was right in the middle of a world's-gone-crazy-with-Coronavirus workweek. Nothing was the same, and yet everything was the same—if you can understand what I mean, because you remember what that felt like. The future was a giant question mark, and fears of the unknown abounded. But the everyday needs of human beings without COVID didn't stop, and that was especially true down in the trenches of the primary care clinics across America. For it was here that I was gifted with the most wonderful reminder from a patient (*without* COVID) that really put things into perspective for me—and was so profound under the circumstances that I cannot help but share his story.

Mr. Smart* is in his 80s and had come to see me for a hospital follow-up visit. First, he had been hospitalized with pneumonia from Influenza and a flare-up of his COPD or chronic obstructive pulmonary disease (compliments of the infection). Then one week later, he'd been driving around at night and gotten lost. He sat in his parked car near a fence between two strange houses for who knows how long, until a woman found him and called the police. He remembered the woman and two police officers who "looked in my wallet and asked me lots of questions." They called his son who took him to the emergency room. The doctors wanted to evaluate his "altered mental status," but he said no and signed out AMA (Against Medical Advice) instead. "I don't want that CaT scan" he told me, as the memories of his misadventure came flooding back. "I just got confused because it was dark, that's all. It's never happened before." Now it was my turn to evaluate him while his wife chose to stay in the waiting room. I'd seen him twice in clinic previously and hadn't really noticed anything unusual about him before. But today, I figured I'd better screen him for dementia, after I listened to his heart and lungs.

Though he tried his best, Mr. Smart only scored 18 out of 30 on my SLUMS Examination, and I knew he had dementia—even taking into account the fact that he had only completed up to the 7th grade in school. He asked me what I was "going to do with all these questions" I had asked him. "I don't want to get blood work today. They checked me for everything at the hospital" that first time, he made sure to tell me. "And I don't want any medicine. I hardly take any medicine, you know." Now it was my turn to speak. "I'm not going to do anything," I said (other than request a urine sample to rule out a urinary tract infection, to which he later agreed). "I just wanted to know where you're at. There are no consequences for any incorrect answers," I reassured him.

Soon, I saw him relax, and then he began to talk. "Jesus is my everything—my all in all," he announced, seemingly randomly. I nodded, and he continued. "This world is just temporary, you know. The only thing that matters here is Jesus, and He's gonna give us a future that's eternal."

"You're exactly right," I smiled, as I thought about the irony of the whole situation. It felt as if I was experiencing a scene right out of God's famous "Backwards Kingdom."[1] The kingdom where the King gives up the adoration and riches of His perfect home and agrees to come to the one dark place where He knows He'll be denied, mocked, and killed. The kingdom where the King actually washes the dirty feet of His servants and teaches them that the first shall be last, and the last shall be first in a world where fame, title, and status don't matter.

In today's episode of "The Backwards Kingdom" that I've come to love, a man with dementia and a 7th grade education is the wisest one of all. In a world where the Stephen Hawkings[2] are revered, and the friends of the Creator are often looked down upon, this veteran hadn't forgotten that "the fear of the Lord is the beginning of wisdom" (Proverbs 9:10 NIV), and that, "Only fools say in their hearts, 'There is no God'" (Psalms 14:1 N LT).

By this world's standards, his brain is failing. But by Heaven's assessment, his mind is still perfect in the only way that truly matters. "Are we done now? Can I go?" he asked hopefully. "Yep, we're done now," I promised him, as I opened my door. Good-bye, wise man from "The Backwards Kingdom." Good-bye.

*Name changed to protect the privacy of my patient

CHAPTER THREE

CARSON AND THE BEARDED DRAGON

"IF YOU THEN, BEING EVIL, KNOW HOW TO GIVE GOOD GIFTS TO YOUR CHILDREN, HOW MUCH MORE WILL YOUR HEAVENLY FATHER GIVE THE HOLY SPIRIT TO THOSE WHO ASK HIM!" LUKE 11:13 NKJV

I hate bugs. And when I say that I hate bugs, I mean that I **really** hate bugs. Eww. Gross. I'm shuddering a little even now just *writing* about bugs. I did like lady bugs for a while. I even dressed my girls in clothes with cute lady bug prints on them when they were toddlers. But then my love for lady bugs waned quickly after they invaded my office for two long years. They lived in the overhead fluorescent lights. They took over my windowsills, office furniture, and carpet. Live ladybugs would even find their way into my food. Almost daily, I had to scrape countless dead lady bug carcasses from the windowsills into the trash can. Of course, we let the landlord know, and they paid for pest control. But the pests were far from controlled.

Cockroaches are even worse. I've never thought that they were cute and neither has anyone else, as far as I know. At least I've never seen children's clothing with cockroaches embroidered on them. When Carson was little, he loved to play a game that we called "Scareds." "What are your scareds?" he used to ask me each night, as we played the game at bedtime. I would let him go first, and he would list killer-creatures in various orders: sharks, lions, cheetahs, and bears. Then it would be my turn, and I always said the same thing: cockroaches and big furry spiders. Yep, I'm more afraid of little ugly creatures that might cause me to scream to death than big, far-better looking ones that can potentially tear me to shreds. And my son thought this was hilarious.

As is usually the case with phobias like mine, there's a background story. Mine dates back to 1990 when I was in the 8th grade. We had just moved to Orlando, Florida and were renting our first home while waiting for our house in Massachusetts to sell. I got up one night to use the bathroom and kept the lights off as usual. Suddenly, I felt something on my hand, so I figured I'd better turn on the light. My hand slid across the wall until it finally located the light switch. Knowing what I know now, I wish it hadn't, because the light revealed my nightmare! Too many cockroaches to count were crawling up and down the walls close beside me. There was no escape. Even worse was the fact that *these* particular cockroaches had apparently learned how to fly! I would later learn that these were Floridian palmetto bugs. Needless to say, I was traumatized—even though I ultimately escaped to the safety of my bedroom and mysteriously, the "flying cockroaches" were nowhere to be found the next morning.

Fast forward to the summer of 1998, and you would find me *wishing* for twenty or thirty flying cockroaches to surround me rather than the far more horrifying reality that I was faced with instead. I had parked my car in a parking garage in downtown Nashville and gone upstairs to study for my MCAT (Medical College Admissions Test) with the Kaplan test prep company in the building above, just as I did each weekday morning that summer. At the close of this particular business day, I headed back down to the garage-level floor to get my car and drive home. Easy task—or, at least, it should've been. Instead, what I found would both shock and horrify me. The garage floor was literally *carpeted* with bugs. No longer could I even see the light-colored concrete beneath. All that was visible were layers and layers of dark bugs.

While I could appreciate that they had come to the shaded, cool garage to escape the humid, summer heat outside, I still felt like I was a character in a creepy horror movie. The fifteen feet that stood between me and my getaway car may as well have been fifteen miles. I stood there frozen like a statue for five long minutes—and then ten more—as I wondered how I was ever going to make it home. Eventually, I decided that I simply had to leave—whatever it took. I braced myself and then began to walk on my tiptoes like a ballerina in an attempt to walk on the very scarce areas of bug-free concrete floor that I could still find. In spite of my best efforts, I heard disconcerting *crunching* noises with every step.

Even after I made it to my car, I knew that the battle wasn't over. Somehow, I would still need to find a way to get past the bugs that were flying around my door and crawling on its window. Too afraid to give the garage floor bugs an opportunity to crawl up my legs, I quickly unlocked my car with the key in hand and opened the door as fast as I could. Once inside, I slammed the door and shuddered. But I wasn't safe yet. I noticed that a couple of the bugs had followed me. Still in shock, I smashed them instinctively with whatever objects I could find.

As I pulled out of the garage, I turned the radio up so that I couldn't hear the crunching of exoskeletons that I knew would otherwise be audible. Outside in the sunlight, I discovered a few more bugs on my windshield. I assumed that they would fly away once I got onto the freeway, but they held on for dear life, even as I drove at least 70 miles per hour. Thinking that I could scare them into flying away by turning on my windshield wipers, I did so. But alas, they stayed put and became smeared bug guts on glass. I would later learn that these bugs were cicadas and made their appearance only once every thirteen years. For months on end, I found cicada carcasses in the trunk of my car.

So, I think you get the point by now. I'm not a fan of bugs. And I've done what I could to secure a bug-free existence for the past two decades with a pretty good success rate. What I *didn't* count on was having a child one day who would ultimately ask me to change that. I have left my comfort zone, that much is certain. But in order to explain, I will need to take you back to another beginning—this one from 2018.

"Mom, can I have a bearded dragon?" nine-year-old Carson asked casually one day. The first time I heard this question, my answer wasn't unexpected. "No, Honey," I answered quickly—almost reflexively. Bearded dragons are lizards. And lizards eat bugs—**live** ones. It wasn't just the bug diet that influenced me, either. I wasn't even sure that the bearded dragon himself would be any less creepy than the creatures he eats.

Although Carson heard my verdict, he didn't exactly look like a boy whose hopes had been dashed, and I wondered why. Soon enough, I figured out the reason. He hadn't given up. "Mom, can I have a bearded dragon?" my son asked over and over as the weeks went by. "No, Honey," I responded each time, never intending to change my mind. *I can resist him,* I thought confidently, determined to stand my ground. No bug-eating creature was going to share my home.

As time passed, I learned the reason for my kid's interest in reptiles. His teacher had lots of them and even used them as rewards. When given the option, Carson would choose holding Mrs. Hyde's bearded dragon during class over any other prize that she had offered. And it didn't stop there. When Christmas time rolled around, my annual made-in-class "mom gift" was a laminated picture of a smiling Carson holding a bearded dragon on his shoulder, along with a message for me beneath. I cannot remember the message but I will never forget the picture.

My son's pleas for his burning desire continued. In church one day, he showed me a folded paper game that he'd made and asked me to play. You might remember creating a similar "origami fortune cookie" to pass the time when you were in elementary school, with its random number choices and hidden future destinies inside. Who would you marry? What career would be yours? It all depended on which number you chose and what lie behind each paper "door." I played round one and waited to see what my fortune would be—only, it wasn't exactly a fortune. Instead, it was a request: *Buy Carson a bearded dragon.* I had to laugh. *What are the odds that I would choose that particular outcome on the very first try?* I wondered. "You wanna play again?" Carson invited. "Okay," I agreed. I chose one of the other three number options this time. But my "fortune" was the same—another instruction to *buy Carson a bearded dragon.* Round three? *Buy Carson a bearded dragon.* Round four? *Buy Carson a bearded dragon.*

I thought about trying to pacify my son with a turtle instead—a Russian or Greek tortoise who would happily eat fruits and vegetables for the rest of its life. But eventually, I realized that it might not be wise to give a nine-year-old a pet who could possibly outlive him. As Carson's tenth birthday neared, I was reminded by my colleague at lunch one day that his wife actually *bred* bearded dragons for a living. And something changed inside this parent who ultimately had the power to either make her child's dream come true or crush it. My heart softened. I stepped outside my comfort zone to brighten the life of the child I love, and it was worth every bit of inconvenience and discomfort that would follow. I will never forget the day that Carson first met Thorn. As he held his very own baby bearded dragon on his shoulder, he announced with heartfelt sincerity, "I *love* him!"

When I imagine how my own Heavenly Father must feel when I ask Him for something I deeply desire, I cannot help but view things differently now. For years, I believed that I had to ask God for the same thing over and over in order to prove myself worthy of the gift that I wanted. And the Bible does encourage us to be persistent with our prayers. In the book of Luke (18:3-5 NLT), Jesus tells the story of a judge who finally gives a woman what she's been begging for—not because he cares about her or her crisis but because he's getting sick and tired of her pleas. "A widow of that city came to him repeatedly, saying, 'Give me justice in this dispute with my enemy.' The judge ignored her for a while but finally said to himself, 'I don't fear God or care about people. But this woman is driving me crazy. I'm going to see that she gets justice, because she is wearing me out with her constant requests.'"

I took this story of my Savior's to heart but realized only years later that I had actually missed the *most* important point. Beyond the fact that the woman's persistence paid off lies a hidden gem—our Heavenly Father is nothing like this selfish judge. We don't have to plead with Him to care about our requests. He doesn't respond simply because we have finally annoyed Him one too many times. Yes, the more often we come to Him, the happier He gets. But we don't have to come to Him repeatedly just to get Him to act. Our God hears us the first time. He even knows what our needs and desires will be before *we* do.

I may have been more like the self-centered judge than I care to admit as a parent. After all, my biggest weakness is selfishness, and it nearly cost my kid his dream. But in the end, I proved to have a little bit of my Heavenly Father in me as well. My child got the bug-eating friend he had persistently requested of his bug-fearing parent. And you know what? It felt good for this mama to make my son's wish come true. So, how much more does Your Heavenly Father desire to give *you* good gifts?

The Bible provides the answer: "Keep on asking, and you will receive what you ask for. Keep on seeking, and you will find. Keep on knocking, and the door will be opened to you. For everyone who asks, receives. Everyone who seeks, finds. And to everyone who knocks, the door will be opened. You parents—if your children ask for a loaf of bread, do you give them a stone instead? Or if they ask for a fish, do you give them a snake? So if you sinful people know how to give good gifts to your children, how much more will your heavenly Father give good gifts to those who ask him" (Matt. 7:7-11 NLT).

Luke tells us in chapter 11, verse 13 (NLT) that the Holy Spirit is one of these "good gifts." So, don't forget that the best gift our Heavenly Father can give us may not be the one that we asked for. It may be better—even though we can't see it. Sometimes, *we* may be the one asking for a seemingly-good stone or serpent when what God really wants to provide for us is bread or fish.

CHAPTER FOUR

FAITHFUL EVEN WHEN WE WON'T REMEMBER

"COMMIT YOUR WAY TO THE LORD, TRUST ALSO IN HIM AND HE SHALL BRING IT TO PASS." PSALMS 37:5 NKJV

I had been frustrated about a certain matter at work for a couple of weeks. There had been no resolution, in spite of my efforts and even the help of my faithful advocate, Ann. I was especially irritated because it seemed to me that the roadblock that I had encountered should have never been present in the first place. The more we tried and failed to fix the problem, the more annoyed and anxious I became. We didn't even know what avenue to take next and simply felt stuck.

Far later than it should have, a thought suddenly came to me. *Why was I allowing frustration and worry to come into my heart over this matter in the first place? Why hadn't I simply taken the matter to my Heavenly Father as soon as it became apparent that my own efforts were never going to be enough?*

Is there any matter that concerns me that is too small for God to care about? Is there any matter that is too difficult for Him to handle?

Still feeling pretty foolish for forgetting the privilege that I have as the (undeserved) daughter of the King of the Universe, I put my irritation and worry aside and simply asked God for help. I prayed and left my immovable earthly problem at the feet of my Heavenly Father three times on that first day, assuming that those would be the first of many prayers. (And that was okay with me.) What happened next was completely unexpected.

Just twenty-four hours after finally deciding to leave the problem in *His* hands, I received word that the matter had been *completely* resolved. And almost as if on cue, my four-year-old actually began to sing, "God will make a way when there seems to be no way."[1] As tears began to well up into my eyes, and gratitude found its way into my heart, I realized that Heaven had done more than answer my prayer and fix the problem I faced. That would have been enough, of course. But I believe that it was actually the Holy Spirit who gave me the idea to ask for Heaven's help in the first place. Even that part was something I needed assistance with, yet it shouldn't have seemed so strange to me. For Jesus is both "the author and finisher of our faith," after all (Heb. 12:2 NKJV).

However, that's not the end of the story. As I was reminded of this experience a few years later, I realized that there was a new lesson to learn from it, and it's a big one. But in order to explain, I must first confess that I have *no* idea what this unsolvable problem was that had apparently stolen my peace. The only thing I can remember is that it related to some business aspect of my private medical practice and that my experienced office manager and I had both tried repeatedly to fix it without success.

With the passage of time, this matter that once seemed so important proved to be so inconsequential that it cannot even be remembered. And this is the new lesson that blows my mind and melts my heart. God knew that my problem from three years ago would soon be forgotten, yet He still took the time to listen to my prayers and intervene on my behalf. Now *that's love*—and just what a parent would do. It must have been a small problem in the grand scheme of things—if I can't even remember it—and yet it sure didn't seem small to me at the time. Isn't that the way it is with our problems as times?

How often do we allow the little things to fill our hearts with anxiety when we have a Heavenly Father who is just waiting for us to ask Him for help? As a wise author named Ellen White once wrote in her book *Steps to Christ*, "Nothing that in any way concerns our peace is too small for Him to notice."[2] How true I have found these words to be in my own life, over and over! Does God always fix the problems I bring to Him as quickly as He did that day a few years ago? Nope. Does He always intervene in the exact way that I'm hoping He will? The answer is no, yet again. But of one thing I am certain: Things will be different because I prayed.

Chapter Five

FLASH'S RESCUE

"'Lord help!' they cried in their trouble,
and he saved them from their distress.
He sent out his word and healed them,
snatching them from the door of death."
Psalms 107:19-20 NLT

L ittle Flash, Makenzie's beloved Siberian gray and white cat, had only just turned one year old when an unexpected accident nearly took his young life. Smaller than the average cat his age—but also far more daring—he typically roams the house with a mischievous spirit that often makes him commit unusual kitty crimes. When he thinks that no one is looking, you might find him stealing bags of marshmallows or hot dog buns and running away with of all his might when he realizes that he's been caught. Or he might decide to drag a bag of lentils with his teeth up the stairs in the middle of the night and inadvertently leave a trail of tiny dried legumes that I'm *still* finding one by one in the oddest places. Other times, you will see him fighting with his much bigger feline brother of the very same age, Tigger. And if you watch closely enough, it will become very clear to you that Flash is the one controlling the rules of their playtime wrestling matches (and that Tigger is quite happy to obey, as long as it means more time in the ring). These are just a few of the many things that "Flashie" has done to make our family laugh.

But Flash is known for more than his shenanigans around our home. He is famous for his affectionate personality too. So often, he can be found snuggling up next to his companions of various species so that he can feel the warmth and comfort that their bodies bring him. And oh, how he craves the belly rubs that prompt him to roll on his back whenever a human being walks by. He certainly wouldn't last without friends for very long.

On one particular morning, however, little Flash found what he thought would be a quiet hideaway to spend some time alone. His secret fort was known only to him, of course, and this set the stage for a tragedy that no one could've predicted until hindsight showed them. As Flash was sleeping, eleven-year-old Carson decided to watch some television on our new reclining sofa. Innocently, he pushed the button that starts the recline process electronically—as he had done multiple times before without a crisis ensuing—and then came the ear-piercing screams of a kitten in harm's way. The details of what transpired next will only truly be etched in the memories of Flashie and the humans who were home that day, as I was at work. But they certainly involved physical and emotional pain, along with terror and helplessness.

Makenzie tried to reach me, but I missed her first attempt. The second time she called, I answered my cell phone and heard these very unexpected words: "Flash is going to die." The tone of her voice was one of heartbreak, mixed with defeat. As the story spilled out, I could hear the frantic voices of my other children in the background. Not only was little Flash seriously injured and in pain, he was also trapped, and there appeared to be no possible way for my husband to free him.

His tail was wrapped around a coiled metal pole that turns like a rotisserie as the sofa moves into the recline position. Even worse, Jason suspected that his tail was broken. Periodically, Makenzie could hear her baby breathing far more quickly than usual. And then there were the intermittent sad and scary sounds he made that were alarmingly unfamiliar.

I did everything I could from afar. I called the emergency veterinary clinic in our hometown. I called our cousin and neighbor, Summer, who is famous for her ability to calmly find a solution to every problem. I even located the phone number for the fire department. After all, if they free cats from trees in storybooks, then surely, they would help a kitten who was in far greater trouble? The volunteer fire station said that making a house call for such a matter would cost us $16,000 and that the fee was out of their control. Summer, on the other hand, didn't hesitate to answer the call for help, and her first order of business was to calm my children.

Once in problem-solving mode, Summer and Jason set out on their mission to dismantle the recliner in a way that wouldn't harm Flash any further. Of course, it involved destruction. But life will always take precedence over material possessions (even when the reclining sectional is new). A full hour later, and Flashie was finally free.

But our relief over his delivery from the recliner that had imprisoned him was quickly dampened by the fact that little Flash obviously wasn't out of the woods yet—physically or emotionally. As Jason and Makenzie rushed him to the veterinarian who was awaiting his arrival, Flash whimpered and panted, and his little heart could be felt racing just beneath his exterior wounds. Once his evaluation was complete, the veterinarian informed Jason that Makenzie's best friend did indeed have a fractured tail, which would require amputation the following day.

Her fur baby's badly-mangled tail was difficult to look at without crying, and Makenzie actually wondered whether he would even find the remainder of his life worth living. Far more heartbreaking was watching Flashie discover the extent of his injury. Over and over, he tried to lick his bloodied, mutilated, and swollen tail—as if he could possibly fix the damage on his own. He knew that he was broken but didn't know how to be the doctor that he clearly needed. And he couldn't possibly know that without surgery and antibiotic therapy, Death would almost certainly be coming for him.

Flash needed to be rescued. It was as simple as that. He needed to be rescued from the recliner. He needed to be rescued from physical and emotional pain. He even needed to be rescued from inevitable infection, sepsis, and death. Clearly, Flashie needed a savior. But it would come at a cost. Although we actually have an insurance plan, the cost of Flash's veterinary bills was still staggering. It would've certainly been easier to pay for euthanasia and buy a new kitten. *Love*, however, said that such a plan just wouldn't do. Flashie was and is irreplaceable. And so, we paid the price.

As the dust has settled, Flashie's rescue cannot help but remind me of my own Savior's choice. We were ruined by sin, and the cost to heal us was infinitely higher than our apparent worth. Creating us cost Jesus nothing, but saving us cost Him and His Father *everything*. It would've been so much easier for them to leave us to our inevitable demise and simply start over again. But alas, their love could not allow them to even fathom such a choice.

Just as with Makenzie's Flash, Jesus and His Father chose the path of incalculable expense for us. We will never be able to pay them back for their seemingly-crazy, love-driven rescue mission any more than Flashie could hope to repay the debt that his own healing required. But as long as we live, we can be grateful. Beyond that, we can choose to shower them with the love that they crave so deeply.

Chapter Six

Heartstrings and Hair Tangles

"As a father has compassion on his children, so the Lord has compassion on those who fear him; for he knows how we are formed, he remembers that we are dust." Psalms 103:13 NIV

I had just gotten home from work and saw my fourteen-year-old younger daughter, Makenzie, come into the kitchen. My first thought was to greet her with a hug, and I walked toward her and opened my arms, as I usually do. Unexpectedly, she pulled away. And then, it got worse. "You stink," she announced matter-of-factly. Stunned and hurt, I didn't even know what to say. "Or maybe it was Charley," she offered next. *Really*? She couldn't tell the difference between my scent and the body odor of our bug man who had been in our home earlier the same day? I argued with her, of course. What woman wants to be the stinky mom in her kid's eyes? "I don't stink," I declared in my defense, as I secretly hoped that my claim was true. "I take my personal hygiene very seriously, thank you very much," I added for emphasis.

But just when I thought that the conversation couldn't deteriorate any further, Makenzie made an accusation that bothered me much more: "You're mean." Her words hung in the air, as I thought about them. I knew that she was wrong (at least, I *hoped* she was), and yet this particular dagger still felt extra sharp. Her older sister, Meliah, came to my defense. "Mom isn't mean. You are."

I told Makenzie that she had hurt my feelings, but she didn't seem to care. At some point, I gave up and went to my room, feeling like the dejected loser of an ambush. Although I didn't want to be known for B.O. *or* meanness, my daughter's words had hurt my heart far more than my pride. Lately, there had seemed to be an unwanted distance between us. The past few times that I had initiated hugs, Makenzie had offered back only side hugs while looking away. Already, I had been missing the tight bear hugs we used to share, as I thought longingly about my memories of our past closeness. Flashbacks of my affectionate little girl spun through my brain like a movie reel.

This not-so-little girl had actually rejected my hug. *How did we get here?* I wondered sadly, with an uncomfortable feeling in my chest. I desperately wanted to go back to the past and be wanted by my child once again. Memories of better times filled my thoughts. As a little girl, she had followed me everywhere, so I nicknamed her Little Lamb. She then decided to call me Mary Mama (because my smart baby knew that Mary had a little lamb, of course). How many times did we watch the "Madame Blueberry" episode of *VeggieTales* together while cuddling? Or play haircut and Kenzie's Kafe? I thought about the pink teddy bear she'd given me years earlier and even named Love Mommy. My heart ached. *Oh child, do you realize how much my happiness and peace are tied up with your love?*

The next day, my teenage Makenzie acted as if nothing had happened the day before. She talked about random things and asked me casual questions.

But there was no apology . . . or hug. I was still hurt. Did she need me only for the things I can give her? I didn't want to give her the silent treatment like a school-age girl—I'm supposed to be a mature parent after all—but I still felt unable to look her directly in the eye. And so, I answered her questions while pretending that I needed to look in a different direction.

That night, it occurred to me that this is how I must make my Heavenly Father feel far too often. *How many times have I failed to give Him the time and affection that He craves, while continuing to ask Him for everything I think that I need?* One of the things that has always struck me most about the Old Testament is how desperately God wants our love and loyalty. He has everything we could possibly want and dream of, and yet He wants a monogamous relationship with us even more. Long before we experienced jealousy and heartbreak for the first time when faced with a cheating partner or disloyal friend, *God* felt that pain. Jason, always the peacemaker, suggested that I simply tell Makenzie how I felt. I knew that he was right, but I still went to bed that night without trying.

The following afternoon at work, I noticed that I had missed a call from Makenzie. As I tried to imagine what she might be calling about, my phone rang again. This time, I answered. "Hello? Makenzie?" At first there were no words—only tears, as she cried. But then the story spilled out. There was a large tangle in her hair that she couldn't get out. "Even Meliah tried to get it out, and she couldn't. She said that I'm going to have to cut it out. It's one-third of my hair, Mom. I'm gonna be bald!" she added for emphasis, before the sobbing started all over again. Although it was a small matter in the grand scheme of things, I knew it felt **gigantic** to my child. And while my own feelings were still hurt from the comments she'd made earlier in the week and hadn't apologized for, I couldn't help but feel empathy for her plight and wonder: *Is this how God feels when I come to Him with my own tears after ignoring Him for a while?*

I knew what I had to do—what I *wanted* to do. I wanted to fix my child's problem and make her tears stop. Although I couldn't see the tangle, I was determined to make things right for my Makenzie, so I tried to reassure her. "I'll get the tangle out, Honey. You won't have to cut your hair. It'll be okay." She didn't sound convinced. "But what if you can't?" Her lack of trust in my ability probably should've insulted me further, but it didn't. My thoughts drifted back to my relationship with my Heavenly Father. How many times had I asked Him for help and then clung to my anxiety and pessimism anyway? Again, I told Makenzie that everything would be okay, even as I prayed silently that it would be. *Please help me to keep my promise, Abba.*

Normally, I never leave work undone before going home—even if that means I'll have to stay hours past my shift. I feel better knowing that the next day's work will be its own, rather than an accumulation of tasks from days' past. But this day, I broke my own rule to get to my child faster. As I left at 5:20, I texted Makenzie, "I'm leaving work now. I'll be home to help you soon." There was no reply.

When I finally arrived, I found a worried teenager in her room, lying on her bed in defeat. "I'm home," I announced loudly, in an attempt to break through her cloud of discouragement. I had planned to tackle the job at hand on Makenzie's bed, but Meliah suggested that we all go to my room instead. First, I went to her bathroom and collected the various brushes and combs that the girls had already attempted to fix the problem with on their own, including Makenzie's favorite pink and black detangler. Next, I sat behind my child and surveyed the damage. This tangle was a *beast*. I started my battle with it by utilizing my usual trick: begin brushing from the very bottom.

I thought about the biggest difference between God and me as a parent. God is *always* capable of fixing the problem (although that doesn't mean that He should or will). Me, on the other hand? Not so much. I hoped that my determination would somehow make up for my lack of physical skill.

When my initial attempts proved to be fruitless, I left in search of my detangling spray. It wasn't underneath my bathroom sink where I normally keep it, and I quickly realized that Meliah had already tried it. I found the bottle in the kids' bathroom and brought it back to the battleground anyway. I grabbed my tweezers and took them to the battle too, because I clearly needed more weapons. Once I had literally soaked her hair with the detangling spray and discovered that neither the tweezers nor the combs and brushes were going to be very helpful, I began to tackle the beast with my bare hands. The process was very tedious—and only intermittently successful—but I found that if I separated strands of hair from the tangled mass and pulled them sideways, then slowly but surely, the tangle continued to shrink.

In spite of my attempts to inflict as little pain on Makenzie's scalp as possible and keep her wincing at a minimum, her tense neck muscles told me that her head was still in full defense mode. I confessed to her that the tangle was worse than I had imagined. But I also told her that it could've been worse and that even hours of discomfort on my bed would be better than several months of waiting for her hair to grow back (should we give up and decide to cut it instead). Mostly, however, I worked in silence as the minutes passed . . . and passed. After nearly an hour, all signs of the beast were gone, and in its place were the same strands of corn silk hair that my Makenzie has had since she was at least two years old. My job as a parent was done, and my daughter was actually pleasantly surprised that the task hadn't taken even longer.

I wondered what would happen next, as I tried not to get my hopes up. But I needn't have tried to protect my heart, and I didn't have to guess for very long. Within seconds, Makenzie threw her arms around me and said, "Thank you!" We hugged tightly for longer than I thought she would allow, and then she offered up the apology that soothed this mother's bruised heart. "I'm sorry, Mom," she simply said, trusting that I would know why.

My response was one I know that my Heavenly Father—who is *full of feelings*—would like **me** to remember the next time I am tempted to pull away from Him or put Him down. I candidly said out loud the words that had been repeated in my head so many times during the past two days. "Do you realize how much my happiness and peace are tied up with your love?" Makenzie nodded, although I'm still not sure that a child—including me—can ever truly understand this reality. Perhaps my kid at least understood well enough to feel the need to explain the reason for her earlier behavior. "You didn't stink," she clarified (thank goodness). "I just didn't want to hug you because I was in a bad mood." Abba Father, help me to do the same for You....

CHAPTER SEVEN

HOT PEPPER SISTERS

"BUT HE WAS PIERCED FOR OUR TRANSGRESSIONS, HE WAS CRUSHED FOR OUR INIQUITIES; THE PUNISHMENT THAT BROUGHT US PEACE WAS ON HIM, AND BY HIS WOUNDS WE ARE HEALED." ISAIAH 53:5 NIV

I was on vacation at the beach in Ocean City, Maryland, watching a random television show in my hotel room. My husband had been channel surfing and stopped when he saw a game show that challenges teams to do difficult, unpleasant things for prize money. It was the first and only time that I watched this particular show called *Don't,* but I will never forget it.[1]

Four sisters showed up for the game, and all of them were potential winners. But interestingly, only one of them was required to do the horrible task at hand. "Eat this hot pepper," the game show host instructed the family's chosen sister, Elena, with a devious smile. "If you can do it without pooping or vomiting," he added with a laugh (as *we* laughed too), "you and your sisters will get $20,000." She did it successfully as her excited siblings watched, and then the next challenge came. There would be another cucumber-sized pepper to eat, but this one was even hotter. And to make the challenge even more difficult, a game show staffer brought out a large glass of ice water and placed it on a small table next to Elena. If she could eat the pepper, she and her sisters would earn another $20,000. But if she drank the water afterward, there would be no extra prize money, and her family would even would lose the $20,000 they had already obtained.

Elena didn't exactly look *normal* after eating that first large hot pepper, but she still appeared capable of moving on to the next round. Her sisters nervously cheered her on. After she was halfway done with pepper number two, the expression on her face began to change to one of discomfort. She glanced at the enticing glass of ice water, and we wondered if she was going to give in, but after a moment of consideration, her determination won out. She kept going, with her obviously-worried sisters looking on.

Now it was time for pepper number three. The same game show staffer brought out a glass of milk this time, and the rules were reiterated. Eat this hotter pepper successfully, and Elena would get another $20,000. Drink the milk or water, and she and her sisters would lose half of the $40,000 she had already earned. Elena was beginning to look like she was running a race, and the expression on her sisters' faces was clearly one of concern . . . and guilt. They were all winning, but only Elena was doing the hard work. She finished the pepper and clutched her stomach as the host asked her if she wanted to drink the milk to quench the fire. It was obvious that she did, but her sisters were counting on her. Elena looked at the table holding the tempting glasses of potential relief, and then she looked at her siblings. "I'm ready for the next pepper," she announced defiantly—to both herself and the game show host—as the winnings now totaled $60,000.

As pepper number four was placed in front of a weary Elena, she reached for it with a trembling hand and used her other hand to fan her open mouth. Neither Elena nor the audience members were familiar with the name of this particular pepper, but we all understood that it was hotter than the peppers that she had already eaten. Though she was obviously suffering, Elena kept going, as if stopping simply wasn't an option. She ate this pepper too, though she was clearly in pain, and sweat began to pour down her face. Elena allowed herself to gaze longingly at the water and milk once more and then pulled her now drenched hair up into a pony tail. As she resisted the comfort that her mouth—and entire body—desperately craved, the winnings total increased to $80,000.

It was time for pepper number five—**the ghost pepper**—if she would consent to be tormented any further, that is. With fear and trepidation—and a body that looked as if it was on the verge of collapse—Elena turned toward her sisters. "You can stop if you want to," they appeared to say with their eyes. "You don't have to do this just for us," her sisters facial expressions tried to tell her so that she would know there was no shame in quitting. But just when we thought that she was about to admit defeat, Elena suddenly appeared determined. Undaunted, she ate this pepper more quickly than the others, as if to get it over with before she could change her mind. And then she lifted both arms up in victory and smiled for the first time in many minutes. Realizing that she had won the battle for them, Elena's sisters began to dance and scream for joy in unison. For all of the suffering that their sister had endured, the prize was now theirs.

I don't remember Elena simply because her experience with the peppers was amusing—although it was, of course. Instead, her story stays with me because it reminds me of my Jesus. Like Elena, He endured suffering so that others could reap the benefits. And just as Elena's sisters don't deserve the gift she paid for with her misery, I don't deserve the eternal life that my Savior's painful sacrifice bought me. Why did Elena do it? I suspect that the answer is love. Love for her sisters, yes. But also, the love of money. And who can blame her? Who doesn't want to win $100,000?

It is here where the two stories diverge. We will never know if Elena would have endured the peppers if the prize money was to go to her sisters alone, and the only joy she would receive is the company of her happy siblings. Perhaps. But with Jesus, we know for certain. Instead of consenting to be tormented in the hopes of gaining riches, He agreed to leave all of His riches behind and suffer—so that we wouldn't have to. Think about it. I did.

CHAPTER EIGHT

IS THIS ALL THERE IS?

"THESE ARE THE WORDS OF THE TEACHER, KING DAVID'S SON, WHO RULED IN JERUSALEM. 'EVERYTHING IS MEANINGLESS,' SAYS THE TEACHER, 'COMPLETELY MEANINGLESS!'"
ECCLESIASTES 1:1-2 NLT

A couple of years ago, I had a patient ask me with all sincerity if "this is all there is" in life. Our clinic visit had begun with the usual pleasantries. "How are you? How have you been?" I ask these questions more times per week than I can count, just as you probably do. Most often—as we all know—this typical greeting is almost always answered positively, whether it's true or not. "Fine," we reply. "Thanks for asking," we sometimes add in order to fill the awkward silence because we know that our response was far too brief and generic.

For these reasons, I wasn't expecting the conversation with my patient to unfold in the way that it did that day. His reply was genuine to its core. And it is one that I will never forget. "Everything is so bad in this world these days and people are awful, and it's only getting worse. Is this really it for us? This is all there is?" With the deep question in my lap, I looked him in the eye and said, "There is only one answer to that question."

Surprised that I would even be able to answer the question at all, he leaned forward with peeked interest. "Yes, this is really all there is for us without Jesus. He's the only answer to that question. It's the whole reason that He came down here to this awful sinful world to die for us." And then I added, "I don't usually preach to patients, but when you asked that question, there was really only one way that I could answer it." He went on to share that he is "basically an atheist," and I felt a burden to convince him of what I know to be true without a doubt.

But I didn't really know how, and I wasn't confident that I could change his mind even if I did. I felt inadequate. Inept. I regretted that I didn't have ready one of those scholarly remarks that are filled with facts from history and science that can't be easily disputed. Surely, a reply like that would remove all doubt from his mind. Except, I wasn't prepared with the perfect pastor-like response.

And so, I dug into my heart and tried to reach him that way instead—with a rope being thrown from one sinful earth dweller to another. I told him that I know Jesus personally, and He has done so many things for me that the random world could never explain. I shared with him that Jesus is the only reason I have peace and joy every day and that everything in this world is meaningless without Him.

Sadly, it didn't surprise me when he told me about the Christian hypocrites that he has come into contact with over the years, just like so many of my other patients have also mentioned. I reminded him that at the end of the day, even Christians are sinful humans who will often let us down. I told him that Jesus is the *only* One we can look at and trust with our hearts. He is the only One in church who truly cares more about our well-being than His own.

Just last week, another patient ultimately asked the same universal question about the meaning of life that we all ask ourselves at some point—even if we don't do it out loud. When I inquired about his mood, he answered me in a different way than most patients do. "There's nothing to look forward to," he replied to summarize his general outlook on life in response to my probe about his mental health. "I don't want to kill myself or anything," he reassured me, although I hadn't asked about suicidal thoughts yet. And then he repeated his previous announcement for good measure. "There's just nothing to look forward to."

Unable to work following a stroke five years earlier, yet still able to complete the basic activities of daily living, his days were spent doing something that most teenage boys could only dream about—playing video games in the basement of his mother's house. Day in and day out, he ate, slept and played video games—but he wanted more. "I don't have a wife or kids," he explained. "What's the rest of my life going to look like? Playing video games?" The fact that he wasn't fulfilled was obvious to both of us. But only I knew that the purpose he was missing wasn't actually marriage or parenthood, as he thought it might be. I could've kept this insight to myself. Our visit wouldn't have taken as long, and he certainly wouldn't have known the difference.

But I felt that he deserved to know the truth. So, I told him. "I have a wonderful husband, four fantastic kids, and a great job. I know how blessed I am to have all of these things, and they do bring a lot of happiness to my life," I acknowledged, before getting to the heart of the matter. "They aren't the reason that I have the courage to get up in the morning or have peace in my heart though," I clarified on my way to the punch line. " *Jesus* is."

He didn't seem convinced—and I had more to say, so I kept going. "I don't know what your spiritual background or beliefs are, but Jesus loves you just as much as He loves me. So, you can have the same meaning in your life that I do. It's my job to take care of you medically and to help you to be as well as you can be. I'll continue to do that—but in the end, you and I are both going to die."

At this point, he nodded in acknowledgment of this morbid and familiar reality, as the clock on the wall said that it was past time to go. There was only one thing left to say this day. "I wanted to give you something that's more lasting and not just keep my secret to myself." A smile developed on his face as we both stood up to say good-bye. And it looked *very* good on him.

Chapter Nine

JOSE

"For our light and momentary troubles are achieving for us an eternal glory that far outweighs them all. So we fix our eyes not on what is seen, but on what is unseen, since what is seen is temporary, but what is unseen is eternal." 2 Corinthians 4:17-18 NIV

It started out like any other morning drive to work. Flipping the radio channels back and forth in an attempt to avoid commercials, I settled on one of my favorite Christian music stations. The usual DJs were taking calls from listeners in search of different—and hopefully entertaining—responses to the same question. Each caller was tasked to finish the same sentence in their own unique way. And they all started their sentence with these words: **"I've never gone this long without...."**

Since we were in the early months of the COVID-19 pandemic, and many businesses were considered "non-essential" in our country's initial shut down, there was a certain humor and familiarity to each caller's answer. "I've never gone this long without going to the dentist to get my teeth cleaned," the first man announced. "Hmm," I said out loud in my car before the running commentary inside my brain chimed in. *That may be true for this guy, but I'm sure that there are plenty of people who have gone this long without a visit to the dentist—long before the pandemic gave them the perfect excuse!* "I've never gone this long without going to church," a woman said next, somewhat sadly. I nodded in agreement, although I knew that no one could actually see me. So many of us could relate to that one. How strange it had been to stay at home and watch the church services of an empty sanctuary from the television in our living rooms, week after week. "I've never gone this long without putting gas in my car," the third listener reported. *Good answer*, I thought to myself, as I subconsciously graded this caller's response too. *There certainly are a lot of people working from home these days*, I acknowledged. Telework to socially distance—that had become the pandemic's mantra, and the roads had indeed been eerily empty during my own recent morning commutes. "I've never gone this long without getting a haircut," the next caller declared. This time, I actually laughed. We could *all* relate to that one. And the crazy hair pictures had been piling up on social media as our consolation prize.

When the next listener called, I was ready to laugh again, but his words immediately changed the tone of the game. "I've never gone this long without hugging my parents—since they both tested positive," he shared, as he finished the sentence in a way that I don't think any of us were expecting. A lot of people had been putting off visits with their parents and grandparents in order to protect them from the virus, but not many could say that both of their parents were already infected at this early point in the pandemic.

One of the DJs made a sympathetic comment in response to the news already delivered—but even more unexpectedly, the caller hadn't told us the worst part yet. "I lost my father to COVID-19 on Friday. And I can't even hug my mother to comfort her," the mystery man added wistfully.

If a loud gasp could actually be silent, then that's what the next moment sounded like to me on the airwaves. But the DJs didn't miss a beat. Within a second, they responded to the caller's unanticipated comment with condolences for his loss and an offer for prayer. They also asked him how he was doing and got his name. Jose. He accepted their offer to pray for him, of course, but not before answering their question about his emotional welfare with a statement that I will never forget:

"I'm not doing well, but I'll be okay in the grand scheme of things."

I didn't need to wonder what grand scheme he was referring to because there is only one grand scheme that can make a man whose loss is still so new tell the world that he is going to be okay without the slightest hesitation. Yet, the confidence in his voice affected even me. Jose's wound was fresh. It had only been a few days, so he probably hadn't even buried his father yet. And like so many other families during the earlier part of the pandemic, there would be no proper funeral. But he knew that he would be okay. *This.* This is the peace that passes understanding, fellow sin-sick planet dwellers.

Jose has found what we need most: comfort in the middle of the storm—not simply healing when it's finally over and the wounds are years old. This is the one thing we need above all else on this difficult, unchosen journey. There is no place we can buy it and only one place we can find it: the heart of Jesus. I am so grateful to Jose for this reminder. But far more importantly, I am thankful to our ever-sympathetic Savior for the sacrifice that makes this kind of hope possible in the first place.

CHAPTER TEN

LESSONS IN PARENTING

"WE LOVE HIM BECAUSE HE FIRST LOVED US." 1 JOHN 4:19 NKJV

I can't even remember what I had said or done to prompt her accusation, but it stung nonetheless. "You always take her side," my fourteen-year-old daughter declared, looking in the direction of her older sister. "I know you like her better than me," Makenzie said next, holding nothing back. "No, I don't," I shot back, attempting to defend my honor as a mother. "I love all my children the *same*," I added to my rebuttal for good measure.

Unconvinced, Makenzie began to walk away from me. "Come back," I asked, as nicely as I could that first time. "No," she said boldly as she continued to walk away. "Come back here," I demanded (admittedly *less* nicely the second time). "No," she dared to tell me again as she turned the corner and actually left the room. My mother-in-law was watching while I failed to command any respect from my child, and I felt like a failure as a parent. More than that, I felt hurt.

Makenzie's phone was taken away in punishment—but in her stubbornness (which she may or may not have learned from me), she pretended not to care. Later that night, she came to my room to ask for the phone, and I told her that I was waiting for an apology. Instead of giving me the apology I craved, Makenzie doubled down on her lack of concern for the phone. "I don't need it," she announced as she walked away again. The next day, we didn't speak, and my husband got caught in the crosshairs when she finally asked for her phone a second time.

"You owe your mother an apology," Jason informed her. "No, I don't," she responded matter-of-factly before countering with, "She owes me one." I bit my tongue and waited for him to handle it, since Makenzie and her father have always been very close, and she usually listens to his advice. I could never have predicted what happened next. The more he argued with her, the more she argued back. And when he finally threatened more punishment, she told him she was afraid of him, adding, "I don't care if you hate me."

Of course, her father had never said that he hated her—or even insinuated it—so I decided to step in. "You shouldn't be afraid of your dad," I interrupted. "You started this whole thing. You should be afraid of yourself instead." Surprisingly, she paused and conceded a bit more humbly, "I am," before walking away.

As the evening hours passed, I wondered if I would ever get my apology. Makenzie was wrong, and I was right (this time). *Eventually, she will need my help with something and realize that she had better treat me with more respect*, I assured myself. After all, she had given me a heartfelt apology the last time she had told me no repeatedly just a couple of months earlier.

I walked by Makenzie's bedroom—with its door closed and no signs of light inside—and continued on toward my own room. But suddenly a thought that could only have come from the Holy Spirit stopped me.

You were in the wrong when God made the first move and reached out to you without waiting for an apology. How often have you been disrespectful to Him and received mercy? How many times has God come down to your level when you didn't deserve it, because you could not even meet Him halfway? Immediately humbled, I knew exactly what I needed to do. I needed to reach out to my child instead of waiting for her to come to me—just as God had done for all of us by sending His Son without waiting for us to become worthy (or even acknowledge that we are sinners).

I prayed silently for help as I opened my daughter's door and entered the dark room. My young teenager was lying on her bed, and I couldn't tell if she was sleeping. I turned on her sleep machine and closed her window. "It doesn't lock," I heard Makenzie say. I decided to lay next to her on her bed, and I quickly noticed that she was still wearing her glasses. This discovery told me that she hadn't been able to fall asleep—or was staying awake in the dark intentionally. "Is something going on with you that you want to talk about?" I asked as I tried to break the ice. "No," she replied. "Are you okay?" I tried next. "Yes," she assured me. I snuggled up next to her, deciding simply to be with her in the silence.

A couple of minutes passed, and then I heard Makenzie whisper, "I'm sorry." "I forgive you, Honey," I responded immediately, as God would do for me. But I knew that my girl needed to hear more than that, so I continued. "I don't want you to respect me because I like respect. When you don't respect me, it makes me feel like you don't love me. And I need you to respect me because it's my job as a parent to teach that to you. A kid can't tell their parents no. They just can't. It's my responsibility not to allow that—and if you say it, I'm going to have to stop it. Then we're just going to get into a fight, and I don't want to fight with you. I *love* you."

Makenzie was quiet for a moment and then said, "I love you, too. I'm gonna really try harder to obey." My heart swelled. We lay there together in the dark as I held her arm in mine. "Do you want me to go now, or do you want me to stay?" I asked her. "I don't care. If you want to stay, you can. And if you want to go, that's okay, too," she replied. "I'd like to stay for a few more minutes," I decided out loud. "Okay," she acknowledged. We cuddled in silence until the minutes were up, and then I kissed Makenzie's cheek and squeezed her hand. She squeezed back, and I told her that I loved her once more before I left. The next morning, when I brought her thyroid pill to her, she said, "I love you," spontaneously, and I thought about how differently things might have turned out had I not made the first move as her parent the night before.

I have realized that I never truly understood things from my Heavenly Father's perspective until I became a parent myself. Being an earthly parent has opened my eyes in ways that nothing else possibly could have. How many times have we said no to God? How many times have we thought He hated us or loved someone else more than us when neither of those things were true? How often has God come down to our level and made the first move because He knew that it was the only way that reconciliation would ever happen—even though we were the ones at fault? I am so thankful that God *never* stops knocking on the door of my heart to make things right, no matter how difficult I make it for Him sometimes. No doubt He'd like to do that for you, too.

CHAPTER ELEVEN

RYDER AND THE BROKEN WINDOW

"BUT YOU, O LORD, ARE A GOD OF COMPASSION
AND MERCY, SLOW TO GET ANGRY AND FILLED
WITH UNFAILING LOVE AND FAITHFULNESS."
PSALMS 86:15 NLT

As I was washing the supper dishes following a rare midweek family meal of tacos and homemade chocolate-covered strawberries, I heard Makenzie scream. "Ryder broke a window! It's *really* broken. There is glass everywhere!" First, I winced reflexively. And then came the heavy sigh.

I admit that my first thought wasn't what it should've been as a mother. Instead of worrying about the safety of my children, I thought about the price tag of the repair. *How many unexpected costs can befall one household in the span of one month?* I asked myself incredulously. This wasn't the first, second, or even third high-priced home disaster we had recently experienced. I'd actually lost count.

Just breathe and stay calm, I thought subconsciously, as I headed up the stairs. Ryder was nowhere to be found, and, of course, I knew why. But it was worse than I thought. He wasn't hiding only because he'd broken a window in his bedroom. There was more—and the rest of the story was even more discouraging.

"Ryder pushed Carson into the window," Makenzie made sure to tell me. "He hurt his head," she reported next while I was still in the middle of processing her first announcement. My heart sank. A window could be easily replaced, but a child's soul is a much harder thing to fix when it's broken. Although he was only seven years old, I knew that his character was quickly developing, and each choice he made—for good or for evil—could build upon the previous one and have a lasting impact.

I examined eleven-year-old Carson's head—and after realizing that he wasn't injured—I asked him what had happened. His answer didn't tell me much more than I already knew. Ryder had lost his temper. We experienced moms know that the truth is usually somewhere in between the two versions of the stories we are told, and that fights between siblings usually have *two* active participants. But on this particular night, I was more concerned about my younger child's reaction than whatever his brother had done to trigger it.

It wasn't that I was simply disappointed in my youngest child's apparent lack of control. I was worried. *And sad*. He'd been losing his temper a lot lately, and I feared that if I didn't intervene somehow and help him to change, he might eventually go down a path that he couldn't return from.

As I thought about how to react to Ryder's "crime" and most effectively make him take responsibility for it, all that I could think about was his spiritual wellness. My son needed help, and I needed a plan. *How can I lead this kid to salvation*? I asked myself, knowing that I didn't have the answer. The burden of that responsibility—and my desperate desire for my seven-year-old's ultimate eternal destiny—weighed heavily on my heart. *Is this how God feels about me*? I wondered.

Ryder opened the door to the closet, where he'd been hiding, and cautiously stepped outside. He was already crying for fear of the punishment that was coming. And it *did* come. The movie night that he'd been planning to have with Makenzie was cancelled, and he understood that it was because she no longer felt like spending time with him on this particular evening. Meliah left his room as well.

Jason summoned a nervous Ryder to our bedroom to learn his fate, and when he returned, my seven-year-old literally plopped himself down on the floor at the entrance to his bedroom, landing right on his stomach in tears. "I'm sorry I pushed you into the window, Carson," he announced in a tell-tale manner that told me his apology had been ordered by his father. "It's okay. You don't have to apologize, Ryder," his older brother replied. And I wondered if his response was a mixture of mercy (knowing that Ryder was probably suffering enough) and guilt (knowing that he hadn't been entirely innocent himself).

Although Ryder quickly learned that he would be working to earn money for the new window, he was actually more concerned about the damage that had been done to the relationships with his siblings. "Nobody likes me anymore," he said with the most dejected look I'd seen on his little face in months. "And Carson's not gonna want to play with me in decades and decades," he added for emphasis.

My heart ached for him—for the suffering he was experiencing as a result of his own sin. Even as I wanted him to learn from it for his own future good—to prevent something worse from happening through him and *to him* one day—all I could really think about was how he was feeling right now.

I took him by the hand and led him to Makenzie's room. After knocking on the door and being granted permission to enter, I found Meliah and Carson inside as well, and the three of them were sitting on the floor and putting a 1000-piece puzzle together. "Ryder is worried that no one likes him anymore," I shared. He was too ashamed to look at his siblings, although he craved their approval and affection and wanted to earn it once again.

Carson actually spoke first and reassured him, "I still like you, Ryder." Meliah piped in next. "We still like you. We even still *love* you, but we just need a little break from you right now." Makenzie nodded in agreement. Throughout the encounter, Ryder tried to cover his face and run away. I attempted to hold him in the doorway so they could give him the encouragement that he clearly needed, but his obvious embarrassment and shame just wouldn't allow him to stay. I thanked the kids for trying and closed the door.

As I tucked Ryder into bed and attempted to tell him a story, he covered his face with the sheet. "Please take the covers off of your head and look at me," I instructed him. A few identical requests later, I saw his blue eyes peek out cautiously from beneath the bedsheet. Once I was sure that he was actually listening, I told him about John*. We had attended the same Christian school and church, but somehow—in spite of his Christian upbringing—he had lost his way.

I learned as an adult years later that John was serving a fifteen-year prison sentence for attempted murder that stemmed from a bar fight, and I could hardly believe it. No doubt, the gulf between John and God had been created just one subtle step at a time. "I don't want you to go to prison one day," I explained as I finished the story and wondered if it would have any effect. "This house is a prison," little Ryder announced, and I didn't know whether to laugh or cry.

More than anything else, I wanted my own little boy to remember "the unseen world" that ever surrounds us—the one that the apostle Paul spoke about (2 Corinthians 4:18). "Just as the good angels from Jesus and the

Holy Spirit stand ready to help you and influence you for good, so do the bad angels from Satan stay close by in the hopes of convincing you to do wrong," I taught my son, as Paul and Peter had warned us about in the Bible (Ephesians 6:12; 1 Peter 5:8). I told Ryder that even if his brother or someone else does something mean or unfair, he will always be responsible for his own choices and the consequences that come from them. "You can't change what someone else is going to do to make you angry, but you *can* decide how you are going to react to it." He listened quietly, and I could tell that he was still reeling from all of the disappointing consequences that had already come from his latest decision.

Ryder needed to learn these things, of course, but I couldn't let the lessons end with my warnings about the bad possibilities. After all, he was already experiencing the negative repercussions of his choice. Beyond that, I also wanted him to know that although things feel bad right now, he can still find comfort to help him with the sadness and shame that had unexpectedly found its way into his little heart. "It's not the end of the world," I reassured him. "As long as you're alive and Jesus is alive, there is hope." With these words, I saw him relax a bit, and I headed to my own bed down the hall—but not before adding, "My love never leaves."

Ten minutes later, my little son called out to me from his bed, "Mom, why did you say that you're frustrated that you are gonna have to pay for a new window when *I'm* gonna be working to pay for the window?" My answer came easily this time. "I said that, Ryder, because no matter how much you work, it's never going to be enough to pay for the window. It's going to cost more than you can possibly earn, so I am going to have to pay the difference." Even before the words had all been said, I felt my heart stop in its tracks.

For I know that I am the one who owes a debt of sin that I can never re-pay. It is I who needs a Father to pay the difference. I suddenly realized that this unfortunate chain of events that had interrupted my night, stolen my peace, and even caused me to worry about my child's developing character was already serving a bigger purpose. It had opened my eyes to the things that my Heavenly Father must feel when I am the child, and He is the parent—when I am the one who has broken the window and am suffering the consequences of my own bad choices. How God longs to comfort me in my self-induced misery and shame—and yet desperately wants to heal me from sin even more. "The prison is one of your own making," He clarifies. I am the One who can free you," my Heavenly Father reminds me. And then I hear my Abba lean in and whisper, "My love never leaves."

*Name changed to protect the privacy of the individual

Chapter Twelve

I CAN FIX IT

"BLESSED IS HE WHOSE TRANSGRESSION IS FORGIVEN, WHOSE SIN IS COVERED." PSALMS 32:1 NKJV

It all started with a single scratch. My SUV was just a baby—only two years old—and we hadn't been in our new-to-us home for very long. I'd never had a garage this big before, and I doubt that I ever will again. At least these are my excuses. The truth is that I had simply been careless.

I parked my car just as I had many times before and assumed that I had pulled in far enough. Only *after* I'd pushed the automatic garage door button on my way inside the house did I realize the disappointing truth too late. The unnatural and uncomfortable sound of metal scraping metal reminded my ears of a chalk on a blackboard type of shriek and told me that I had made an irreversible mistake. I knew this to be true before I even saw the damage. And yet I still hoped that my ears had deceived me and I would find my first new car unharmed after all.

Instinctively, I closed my eyes as I rounded the corner, already beginning to wince in anticipation of what I might see—and yet still holding out hope that my ears had deceived me. They hadn't, of course. I wasn't that lucky. When I opened my eyes, I saw the thick, deep vertical scratch that the metal bar on my garage door had loudly carved into the back of my car only moments earlier. My heart sank. How could I have let this happen? If only the accidents in our lives came with a do-over.

The scar was ugly, but I was determined to hide it myself without seeking the assistance of a professional and breaking the bank. A few days later, I rummaged through the papers in my glove box until I found the document that listed the exact name of my SUV's paint color. A quick internet search led me to a company that claimed to be able to match any vehicle's paint color by make, model, year, and factory paint name. I found the products for my 2012 "quicksilver" Buick Enclave easily enough and decided that the painting pen would be the easiest solution. Anxious to cover the scratch that marred my once perfect SUV, I used the pen of promise immediately when it arrived in our mailbox. Soon enough, however, it became apparent that my plan was a bust. I could still see the scratch. It simply looked different now.

I decided that I should've chosen the spray paint version of the matching touch up paint instead—and one more internet purchase later, I was ready to try again. Wanting to be as careful as possible, I thought that it would be wise to cover the unharmed parts of my SUV's back end with cardboard, so that I could limit the spray paint to the area of the scratch. It seemed like a good plan. And to this day, I still don't know why it failed. There is the matter of the imperfect color match, of course, which I discovered too late. But the second round of unintentional damage went beyond a pigment mismatch. After the "protective" pieces of cardboard were removed, I could see the delineation of the different paint colors, and I decided that I should probably add *more* spray paint to blur the edges and blend the two silver colors together.

The result was truly unsightly—far worse than the scratch that had promoted the attempted cover up in the first place. The strokes of the spray paint made the back of my Enclave look like it was in desperate need of a bath. In fact, it reminded me of the dirty, dusty vehicles that compel passersby to write "wash me" in the grime with their fingers. *If only the fix was as simple as a car wash*, I thought more than once over the next few years. That's right. *Years*. I finally gave up and resigned myself to living with the hideous damage that I'd caused.

My defeatist attitude didn't keep me from feeling embarrassed at the thought of strangers believing that I had simply neglected to wash my car. Multiple times each week, those thoughts drifted into my mind. But the money it would've taken to have the Buick dealer fix it always seemed better off spent on something else. So, I learned to live with the visible scars of my mistake instead. Don't we all do that sometimes? We give up on repairing the things we've ruined because the solution just seems too hard?

Years passed. At one point, my father-in-law tried to wash my car for me, thinking it was simply dirty. (What'd I tell you?) When the usual soap and water failed to make it look clean, he tried his "special car stuff" next. I couldn't tell you what the "special car stuff" consisted of—perhaps a heavy-duty car wax of some type? All I know for certain is that it was no match for my spray paint fiasco. And so, my father-in-law gave up too.

One Sunday, I impulsively decided to see if I could remove the dusty spray paint with an SOS pad. I know you can already see the next part coming, but please remember that I felt I didn't have much to lose at this point. And in my defense, this same SOS pad hadn't appeared to hurt my white ceramic farm sink. So why not try it on my less-than-perfect car? I turned on the hose and got to work, determined to scrub my mistake away. Using counterclockwise circular motions and a strength that spawned from my disgust, I scrubbed and sprayed until all signs of my mistakes were g one.

I couldn't believe what my eyes were telling me. My car looked beautiful again! I didn't even care that I could still see the original, deep scratch that had prompted my ill-fated cover-up in the first place. The spray paint—aka permanent, dirty dust portrait—was gone. *Gone*, I tell you!

At first, I was pleased with my apparent good fortune. Who knew that the SOS pad had *this* talent too? I drove to the grocery store excitedly, no longer self-conscious about what a driver behind me might notice or think. After parking, I walked around my car with a skip in my step, excited to catch another glimpse of the beauty that the SOS pad just uncovered. What I found instead wasn't quite as thrilling.

With the water from the hose now evaporated by the sun, I could see a multitude of fine scratches where the ugly spray paint had once been—no doubt left by the SOS pad I had just been praising. Although the scratches were at least preferable to the far more noticeable mistake that the SOS pad had erased, I still felt like an idiot. I should've known that the SOS pad's assistance would come at a cost. My mistakes were multiplying. Each attempt to fix the mistake before it had simply led to another. Do you ever feel like that?

Next, I got it into my head to check the internet for a do-it-yourself solution that didn't involve falsely advertised, far-from-perfectly-matched quicksilver spray paint. I wasn't really expecting a solution. But I stumbled upon a YouTube video that promised to provide one.[1] A man about my age used sand paper squares of varying coarseness to *purposely* scratch a red car door in order to prove his point. When he was finished, the unattached car door looked even uglier than the back of my car. He now had my full attention. The scratches he had created were easily visible. Intrigued, I watched him reach for a can of WD-40. He sprayed it over the scratches and then began to buff the car with a microfiber cloth. Within seconds, the scratches were completely invisible! I was amazed!

Then the skepticism set in. I would believe it when I saw it on my own vehicle. I grabbed a microfiber cloth from my laundry room and drove to the local hardware store to buy a bottle of WD-40. I sprayed it on vigorously, as the words of the man from YouTube replayed in my mind. "The clear oil will fill in the scratches." I closed my eyes as I wiped the extra oil away with the cloth—almost afraid to open them and learn the verdict. Suspense made me look anyway.

As I opened my eyes, I beheld a glorious sight. It worked! My mistakes had been covered! Immediately, the spiritual lessons of my crazy little journey hit me in the face. The scratches had been *my* fault, and each time I had tried to fix them on my own, I had only made them worse. The clear WD-40 oil reminded me of the purity and sacrifice of my Savior, Jesus, who is able to fill in the scratches and cover my sins whenever I am ready to wipe them away. I simply need to decide that they are ugly and want them gone. As is too often the case in our lives as sinners, I waited far longer than I should have—alternating between periods of living with an attitude of defeat and trying to fix my mistakes on my own. We don't have to give up and live with the ugliness of sin. Jesus stands ever ready to cover our mistakes by filling in the scars with his own righteousness.

But there is one important caveat. We cannot simply ask Him once and walk away, forever healed—just as I couldn't fill in the scratches of my mistake with WD-40 one time and hope for lasting beauty. As time passed, I learned that oil eventually evaporates, leaving the scars of my bad decisions visible once again. It turns out that I didn't actually watch the entire YouTube video and had missed the part where the ugliness comes back.

Nevertheless, there was a satisfactory solution. Daily, I infused those scratches on my car with the WD-40—and each day, it made the difference that I hoped for. I cannot help but think about the times when I have allowed the cares of life—or even the unstructured, carefree weeks of vacation—to relegate my Friend Jesus to the sidelines. It is on these days that my imperfections become more apparent—and not only to others but to *me* as well.

There's an inverse relationship between my worst self and my nearness to the Savior. The further I am from Christ, the less you will like me. I'm impatient and selfish. I'm more likely to put others down and less likely to believe that I'm the one at fault. The closer I am to Jesus, the more you will want to be around me. The rough spots—or scratches—in my character become less noticeable because my Redeemer fills them with Himself. I am more loving and generous—and filled with a peace and joy that can easily elude me when I wander too far from the Son of God.

Chapter Thirteen

FLASH'S RESCUE 2

"For the Son of Man came to seek and save the lost." Luke 19:10 NIV

When Survivor Flashie was a year and a half old, he went missing. It was nearly 10 o'clock at night, and I was just about to go to sleep. I glanced at the clock and felt proud of myself for sticking to my resolution to go to bed earlier than usual—something I often have good intentions about doing but never actually manage to accomplish. *This* was the moment my Makenzie suddenly realized that she hadn't seen her beloved cat in several hours, although she had been home the whole time. "I just thought he was napping somewhere all day," she replied defensively, after I asked her why she had only thought about Flash at this late hour. Admittedly, I said this with a frustrated tone of voice that probably insinuated she wasn't an award-winning cat mom. To add insult to injury, I told her that Flash might have gotten outside—and since she hadn't realized that he was gone for several hours, it was going to be too late for there to be any real hope of finding him.

If you're suddenly thinking that *I'm* the one who wasn't an award-winning mom on this particular night, then you would be right. It was nothing other than a giant **Mom Fail**. I knew it as soon as the words came out of my mouth. I could even feel the guilt in the pit of my stomach. Now I had three problems: There would be no early bedtime. My baby's baby was missing. And now my baby almost certainly felt worse than before because the mother who could have comforted her in her distress had chosen to lecture her instead.

With regret in my heart, I left in search of "Flashie Dashie." The rest of the family hunted diligently for him, too. Six humans looked everywhere a feline could possibly go: under the beds, inside the closets, and behind each cabinet door and dresser. But Makenzie's little cat was nowhere to be found—not even in his favorite venue of mischief, the pantry. Our worry g rew.

Remembering that the heating and air conditioning technician had been in the house earlier the same day only made our fears worse. Afterall, his entrance and exit had both served up opportunities on a silver platter for Flash to escape outside into the wild blue yonder should his little feline heart be so inclined. Then, there was his time in the attic itself. Surely Flash would not have climbed up the ladder and followed this stranger into the attic—or would he?

Grampa brought our ladder up from the garage, and, as we all stood by and wondered, Meliah began to climb it fearlessly. "I think I heard something," she announced. "There it is again!" we heard her report excitedly. Was it merely wishful thinking? I didn't know. But Meliah seemed convinced. "It sounds like a tiny meow," she clarified. "I've heard the same sound three times now. I think it's Flash."

Several feet below, Makenzie sat on the floor in an almost crumpled up state—waiting with bated breath for positive news, yet not wanting to get her hopes up. "It *is* him," Meliah burst out with confidence. "He's over there!" Makenzie began to cry with tears that sounded as if they'd come from a mixture of relief and guilt for her little cat's plight.

Finding Flash was only the first step, however. Getting to him wouldn't prove to be so easy. Meliah had to balance herself on the wooden attic beams *without* falling into the cotton candy-appearing insulation, which we knew wouldn't support her weight any better than a cloud. A couple of minutes passed that felt much longer. Then *finally*, the happy announcement came. "I've got him!" Meliah called out in victory, as she headed back to the attic door with the furry prize in hand and handed him off to Grampa who was standing by the ladder below. Eventually, Flash was placed in his little mama's waiting arms.

Normally, the successful rescue would have brought immediate cheers, but our first responder was still in the attic and had suddenly realized that she must come down the ladder without any sensation in her feet to guide the process. Of course, she had climbed into the attic and up the ladder using these same feet only minutes earlier, but it's much easier to be brave in the moments when a hero is urgently needed. Now that Flashie was safe, the distance between the attic floor and top stair of the ladder seemed daunting to one with an impaired sensory nervous system (which is also a story for another day). I climbed to the top of the ladder and held out my hand, but she still looked in my direction with hesitation and said, "I can't feel anything." Her father and grandfather offered to come get her, but Meliah declined the offers and remained frozen with fear until she eventually found the courage to put one numb foot in front of the other once again.

After Meliah was safely on the ground, I turned my attention to Makenzie. She was still crying, and soon I heard her say, "I'm not a good cat mom." My heart sank. "Of course, you are," I tried to reassure her. "You just thought he was sleeping. He does like to sleep a lot during the day," I acknowledged in my younger daughter's defense. "That's why he's so full of energy at night and bounces around your room when you're trying to sleep." She didn't look convinced, and I knew what I needed to do.

I knelt down and put my arm around her as I apologized. "I'm so sorry, Makenzie. You weren't the bad mom—I was. I only said those things because my sleep was being interrupted. I was being selfish." It felt good to acknowledge this reality—even though I wished it wasn't true, and I also knew that it wouldn't heal the wound that I had inflicted on my child's heart. But I wasn't done making amends. Next, I asked the question that I already knew the answer to. "If I hadn't said those things to you earlier, would you have thought of them on your own?" Makenzie looked down before confirming my suspicion. "I don't want to say, because I don't want to hurt your feelings."

Another apology was definitely in order, although it felt like I would simply be trying to dress a deep chest wound with a small Band-Aid. My daughter had forgiven me when I asked, of course, but it was one of those moments when you realize that even the relief of forgiveness cannot undo the seed of hurt you've planted. As I pondered how much better it would have been had I not been so self-centered in the first place, a happier thought came to mind.

This second rescue of Makenzie's little cat, Flash, suddenly reminded me of the fact that our Shepherd Jesus came in search of us and our tiny lost world—out of all of the planets in the universe—just as He went after the one lost sheep in the parable He told while He was here. Our Savior missed us—because we weren't with Him—and went on the rescue mission of all rescue missions, in spite of the fact that He knew it would cost Him everything and even take His life. It was far *worse* than inconvenient for Him, but He did it anyway—without hesitation—because of love. No box office hit or award-winning movie of a reconnaissance mission could ever compare to the real-life story that we're a part of. The rescue of the captives has already been successfully won by Jesus. Satan knows that he has lost the battle and must allow his prisoners of war to go free—*if they want to*. So, the enemy of sinners is counting on one thing: he is hoping that they won't actually want to follow Christ out of the prison camp.

But don't stay, I say! Don't believe the lie that there is more freedom under his command. It's been the trick of an eternal lifetime. Come out of the attic. Your Rescuer has arrived! Take His hand and **never look back**.

CHAPTER FOURTEEN

FORGOTTEN LENSES

"THEN JESUS SPOKE TO THEM AGAIN, SAYING, 'I AM THE LIGHT OF THE WORLD. HE WHO FOLLOWS ME SHALL NOT WALK IN DARKNESS, BUT HAVE THE LIGHT OF LIFE.'" JOHN 8:12 NKJV

I seemed to be trudging through the work day more slowly than usual, but I couldn't pinpoint any particular reason. The work was still getting done, of course, but something felt off. I shrugged off my feelings. It was a Monday, after all. *Everything* seems more difficult on a Monday. I talked to my patients on schedule, playing detective, judge, scientist, psychologist, friend—and even secretary—as I usually do. I stared at my two computer monitors and rode like the wind with my fingers on the keyboard, as is my custom. Nothing unusual happened (although unusual isn't exactly unexpected in my line of work anyway).

The hours passed and the sun went down—which never fails to happen, whether life is easy or difficult, planned or unplanned. As always, an empty clinic left my colleague Taryn and I alone in our offices doing computer alerts, secure messages, and paperwork long after the rest of the employees had gone home. Although Mondays typically bring more after-clinic work than the other weeknights, it still seemed to be taking me longer than usual to get through each task. I wanted to go home, but I had decided years ago that since each day comes with its own responsibilities, I would try never to leave until each day's work was finished. I made myself a second cup of coffee but continued to feel like I was wading through quicksand. Another hour passed.

Finally, I was done with my work and free to go home, knowing that nothing had been left undone (which is always a good feeling). As I was packing up my things, I reached into my purple work bag out of habit and grabbed my glasses case. When I opened the case to put my glasses away, the moment of realization came. There were my glasses, still in the case. I hadn't been wearing them and had gone without my progressive bifocal lenses *all* day. This wasn't the first time that I had forgotten to put on my glasses, of course, but it was the first time that it had taken me an entire work day to notice what I was missing.

How often do we do the same thing with Heaven? We live our lives and look at our world without the lenses that God so desperately wants to give us. And because of this, we miss out on so much. Even worse, our lives are much harder than they need to be. I've discovered that God doesn't give us these lenses all at once, although He's certainly capable of doing so. Our Heavenly Father just isn't in the business of building robots who will love and obey Him simply because they lack free will. So, these **life-saving** lenses can only come to us in the form of vision that we've developed from spending time with Him.

Once I knew the truth, what bothered me most that day wasn't the fact that I had made it harder on myself than it needed to be. By that time, the work had already been done and the hours of life had been spent. What bothered me instead was the discovery that I hadn't even realized I had lost the superior vision *I had already known*. I can still remember the very first time I saw trees through lenses that corrected the astigmatism I'd had for thirty-nine years but never knew about. I was amazed by the appearances of the branches. I was amazed by the details of the individual leaves. Mostly, I was amazed that I had actually thought my vision was already perfect.

Some people know that their vision is blurry because they cannot see anything without their glasses. My husband's prescription surely falls in this category! But for my eyes (which are blinded instead by *wearing* his glasses), it was different. I had never even known what blurry vision was until I started careening toward my forties and could no longer make out the letters on my shampoo bottle. Suddenly, I realized that I was becoming like my parents who had long been holding their menus far from their faces and using magnifying glasses whenever they could get their hands on them.

There had been other work days without my glasses that I lamented almost immediately. So, why hadn't I realized how poorly I could make out the words on my computer screen on this particular day? I don't want to miss the spiritual lessons that are hiding in plain sight here—and I don't want you to miss them either. *There are important realities that will only be visible to us if we develop the lens that allows us to see things as God does.* And that lens can only be acquired from gleaning the hidden treasures that He shows you in His Book or whispers to you during your prayers. Without them, we can't see anything as it really is.

I don't want to be blind to the things, ideas, and meanings that truly exist. More importantly, I want to know when I'm living in the dark. I want the absence of the light to bother me so much that I'm compelled to search for it with all my might. "For this people's heart has become calloused; they hardly hear with their ears, and they have closed their eyes. Otherwise, they might see with their eyes, hear with their ears, understand with their hearts and turn, and I would heal them. But blessed are your eyes because they see, and your ears because they hear" (Matthew 13:15-16 NIV).

CHAPTER FIFTEEN

FLAGPOLES AND BONE MARROW

"I WILL GIVE THEM AN UNDIVIDED HEART AND PUT A NEW SPIRIT IN THEM; I WILL REMOVE FROM THEM THEIR HEART OF STONE AND GIVE THEM A HEART OF FLESH." EZEKIEL 11:19 NIV

On the surface, flagpoles and bone marrow have nothing in common. In fact, two things couldn't possibly appear more different. A flagpole is an inanimate object made of metal. Tall and skinny, it is designed to display a flag—and grow nothing. Bone marrow, on the other hand, is a living tissue within the human body whose job it is to manufacture the cells in our blood. To put it simply, our white blood cells fight infections, our red blood cells carry the oxygen to all of our organs, and the platelets keep us from bleeding to death.

I never saw the two in the same light until we tried to replace the original, worn-out flagpole in the yard of our new home a couple of years after moving in. The house had been built in 1996, and Jason and I suspected that the telescoping pole had been installed at the same time. Initially tall and glorious when we bought the house, it soon began to fall down to shorter and shorter heights. Each time this happened, we would climb a ladder and try to bring it back to its former magnificent height, but our repairs of its locking mechanism never lasted, and we finally decided that it was time for a new flagpole. Buying it was the easy part. When the giant box arrived in the mail, I was naturally excited. But all too soon, I realized that removing the old, damaged pole wouldn't be so easy.

The visible portion above the ground represented only a part of the entire pole—and, although it may have been the bigger fraction of the whole, it was the least important section in terms of its removal. Beneath the ground resided a sleeve that was held strongly by twenty-four-year-old concrete. The only way to uproot the entire flag pole and make room for the new one was to drill through the bonds of cement that didn't want to let it go. And although I wasn't actually the one who performed the task—I can thank Jason and his father for that gift of labor—I *can* tell you with certainty that it wasn't easy! As I thought about it, I was reminded of bone marrow. And since you are probably thinking, "Huh?" right about now, let me try to explain.

When my daughter Makenzie was diagnosed with Myelodysplastic Syndrome (MDS) at the age of three, the normally inconspicuous bone marrow suddenly seemed much more important. The stem cells in her bone marrow had essentially gone rogue. A portion of them had mutated and decided to make strange versions of themselves that weren't able to keep up with the production of her army of white blood cells, red blood cells, and platelets. Because MDS doesn't require treatment as urgently as its more infamous blood cancer relative leukemia, and it also causes death more slowly than leukemia in those who succumb to it, you might think that it would be conquered by chemotherapy more easily. I once did. But alas, the opposite is true.

Makenzie's oncologist, Dr. Haydar Frangoul, once described the two diseases as being different parts of the same tree. Acute Myelogenous Leukemia (AML)—which Makenzie's Monosomy 7 type of MDS inevitably turns into if given enough time—represents the branches of the tree. Myelodysplastic syndrome, on the other hand, is more sinister in the long run because it represents the *roots* of the tree instead. Chemotherapy alone is pretty good at cutting off the branches of the diseased bone marrow tree, but it cannot uproot the mutated stem cells far below the surface by itself. For that task, a complete overhaul is needed. And what a daring feat that is....

In cases of leukemia, smaller doses of chemotherapy can be used—and because the stem cells themselves aren't killed by the lower doses, they are able to replenish the blood cells that were destroyed by the treatment. With myelodysplastic syndrome, higher "myeloablative" doses of chemotherapy are needed to obliterate even the stem cells, eventually pulling out the entire tree by its roots. At first glance, this sounds like a good thing. Why wouldn't you want to pull out the blood cancer by its roots in every case? The reason is simple. If the roots are taken, there will be no way to regrow the tree—no stem cells remaining to replace the blood cell lines that are critical for life—not unless you have some tree seeds waiting in the wings to help you start all over, that is.

The risk of the task lies in the time it takes to grow a new tree—and the fact that there is *no guarantee* that your seeds will even become a new tree at all. While the marrow is without stem cells following myeloablative chemotherapy, the patient is at high risk of developing any number of potentially fatal infections, which the unseen white blood cells we take for granted normally prevent for us. The red blood cells and platelets can be replaced fairly easily with blood transfusions, but the infection-fighting white blood cells can only come from the bone marrow itself. As you can probably guess, this marrow—or seeds for the new tree—comes from a stem cell transplant. And this process is far more complex than a simple blood transfusion. Red blood cells only have to be matched by blood type, while stem cells are ideally matched in ten different ways. A donor with the winning combination or match is sometimes hard to find—and even when you can find them, their stem cells may still decide to attack the recipient's organs (in a process called graft versus host disease—or GVHD—that can occasionally be fatal).

My much-prayed-for daughter came through her myeloablative chemotherapy and stem cell transplantation successfully and is now a healthy teenager, but it was the most trying experience of her life—and mine. The physical and emotional pain that she suffered through—and the heartbreak and anxiety that were her parents' to experience—are indescribable. Even now, I'm still not ready to read the journals I kept faithfully during those dark days. Replacing a flag pole is far easier, of course, and it doesn't come with any comparable danger or anguish. But the similarities between the two remain and remind me of a third "thing" called sin.

Sin too is often inconspicuous, with unseen parts of it beneath the surface. It's like myelodysplastic syndrome, rather than leukemia, and to remove it is much harder than it appears. Cutting down its branches just isn't good enough. The whole thing must be uprooted in order to keep it from quickly regrowing branches that will ultimately come from the same tainted source. A personal decision is involved, along with trust in the help of Another. Just as Makenzie couldn't replace her own damaged marrow without the assistance of two great physicians, and I couldn't replace the old flagpole without the strength of my husband and father-in-law, the root of our sins simply cannot be destroyed without Jesus Christ. He is all of those things for us: the Great Physician, our Helper, and Strength.

Is there risk involved? Sure. You will *die* to self and let go of things that you currently cherish. But the process will benefit you beyond your wildest dreams and ultimately keep you from losing your life. And in the end, when your cold, sick heart of stone and sin has been replaced with a new, healthy heart of flesh and holiness, you will also have found the prize of an eternal lifetime—the very Best Friend you have ever had.

Chapter Sixteen

STUFFED PRINCE

"And I will be your Father, and you will be my sons and daughters, says the Lord Almighty." 2 Corinthians 6:18 NLT

"**D**id you throw away the little rhino?" seven-year-old Ryder asked me unexpectedly. *Guilty as charged*, I confessed only inside my head initially. Earlier in the day, I had spent hours cleaning his messy room, surprisingly finding more trash than toys. Admittedly, there are times when the designation of an item as trash isn't exactly clear cut. Sometimes, the value of an object is simply in the eye of the beholder.

As the beholder during the clean-up process, I had filled multiple trash bags with seemingly unimportant items. *Literal* trash was found in every corner of my youngest child's room, of course—something that no longer shocks a parent by the time they get to kid number four. Then, there were the broken toys, toys with missing parts, and the toys that I hadn't seen Ryder play with in well over a year. By the time that I was done cleaning his room, I was feeling pretty pleased with the job that I'd done. This kid's room looked great, if I do say so myself. I took the garbage bags to the trash can outside and forgot all about them.

Hours later came the question that brought pangs of guilt to this mama's heart. I'd never thought that the tiny stuffed rhinoceros was important to Ryder. I do remember how much his older brother Carson had once wanted a bigger stuffed rhinoceros at the Nashville Zoo years earlier. When the tears of that boy came, I couldn't resist them. They weren't the tears of a child who was throwing a fit in order to get what he wanted. Instead, they had been the tears of a child who felt that he was about to leave behind a friend that he'd already bonded with. The rhino came home with us that day, and Carson named him Rhiney. For a few years, he couldn't sleep without him. And then one day, when he thought that he was too old to sleep with stuffed animals anymore, he allowed Ryder to sleep with Rhiney instead.

I can't tell you where the smaller stuffed rhinoceros came from because I don't remember. Each house I've had since I first became a mother has inexplicably attracted stuffed animals and multiplied them beyond any reasonable number! And so it was with the little rhino, who seemed unimportant—both upon first glance and even after the seconds of consideration that I gave to his value. No memories of either son snuggling with him could be found in my brain so into the trash bag he went. Like so many other toys that hadn't survived my cleansing of a child's room before it, I expected my little son to forget that it had even existed. The purged toys were rarely missed, so why would the small stuffed rhinoceros be any different? Rhiney, on the other hand, easily made the cut (although I can't exactly say whether that was for the benefit of my sons or my own sentimental nature).

Later that same day, Ryder approached me in the kitchen. And then came the unexpected question. "When you were cleaning my room, did you see a *little* rhinoceros?" I knew immediately that I had, of course. *Mom fail. Can't lie.* These are the phrases that burst into my remorseful conscience just before I made my confession out loud—and once I did, I heard the words from my son that really surprised me. "Uhm, he was kind of important. He's Baby Rhiney."

Besides regret, my heart was also filled with curiosity. How could Ryder miss that seemingly unimportant stuffed animal? There was nothing obviously special about him—unlike some stuffed animals whose value is immediately apparent. To look at him, you wouldn't see anything that stood out. No perfect size or cute face. No special colors or especially soft fur. He was just a plain gray rhinoceros, hardly big enough to even cuddle with. That's all I saw.

My son, on the other hand, saw Baby Rhiney as a treasured friend whose worth stemmed from his own love for him, rather than the price that he would sell for at a toy store . . . or a garage sale. The small, ordinary stuffed rhinoceros was precious—not because of who he was but because of *who* declared him to be worth saving. I thought about these things as I searched the trash bags for Baby Rhiney outside in the rain. Nothing could've interrupted my important rescue mission that night, for the unremarkable rhino had suddenly become a beloved prince.

When I finally spotted the prized little rhinoceros, I was too excited to notice that my clothes were now soaking wet. As I raced to reunite my little boy with his cherished Baby Rhiney, the spiritual parallel smacked me in the face. We, too, were once ordinary. Nothing special. Of average worth. In fact, we were *worse* than run-of-the-mill. Satan, our accuser, has actually told God that our sins have made us worthless. We can't argue with him either—at least not with any facts. He's right, after all. We aren't worth saving.

Yet, we are the luckiest beings in the universe. Our story didn't end the way that it was fated to because an Advocate came to our defense. "They are worthy because I am," the Prince tells our accuser. "Their value is infinite simply because *I* love them." And so, we too are rescued from the trash and brought into the palace.

Chapter Seventeen

Who Ate the Missing Cookie?

"But now in Christ Jesus you who once were far away have been brought near by the blood of Christ." Ephesians 2:13 NIV

Once upon a time, there were two dozen cookies. Twenty-four delicious chocolate chip cookies had been baked for Makenzie's sleep over with Sahomy and taken straight from the oven. They were warm, soft, and gooey. And apparently, they were also irresistible.

Seven-year-old Ryder found me in my room, finishing up another chapter in this book before dinner. The cookies had been left to cool on the kitchen island, and my only thought had been to protect them from the girls' cats. "Are the cookies ready?" my youngest child inquired. Thinking like a mother, I knew that there was only one way to answer such a question. "They're for after supper."

The meaning behind my words seemed lost on my young boy. "Yeah. But are they ready?" he asked again with a seemingly suspicious motivation. I decided that two could play at this repeat-yourself game, and that perhaps a little more emphasis was needed this time. "They're for *after* supper." While I didn't exactly get the "okay Mom" confirmation I was looking for, at least he didn't ask me if the cookies were ready a third time, so I took that to be at least a partial parenting win.

When the curry Gramma made for supper was ready, and I arrived in the kitchen, I noticed a glaringly empty spot on one of the cookie sheets. One cookie was missing, and it didn't take a genius to figure out who the guilty party was. I suppose that technically it could've been any one of my four sugar-loving children, but little Ryder was this detective's lead suspect. After everyone had made it downstairs for supper, I made a general announcement. "Who ate a cookie already?" And one by one, they all replied, "It wasn't me."

My fellow parents out there know that at this point, it's not about the cookie anymore. A cookie is valuable, but your kid's honesty is worth a whole lot more. I pulled Ryder aside to give him some privacy before I asked him to tell me the truth. "Did you take the cookie?" I inquired, as I rooted for him to confess. The look of fear on his face was one that I recognized. How many times had I worn it on my own face as a child when I knew that I was about to get caught?

I can still remember instinctively hiding behind my parents' dining room buffet when I was only three years old. In the beginning, my crime had seemed like a good idea, but then there I was—on the run in my own home. I could hear my mom call out from the kitchen, "Who licked all of the icing?" as my newly five-year-old sister stood crying at the sight of her ruined birthday cake. And I was afraid. Denial—as I preferred to think of it instead of lying—seemed preferable to punishment . . . and shame.

With my thoughts back on the present, I could see that I wasn't going to get anywhere with my seven-year-old unless I first addressed his fear. So, I tried to give him an incentive to be truthful. "I'd rather find out that you did something wrong than find out that you did something wrong *and* lied about it. You'd get in more trouble if you lied about it, too," I explained. I could see the wheels turning in his growing first-grade brain, but I wasn't sure that my words would be enough. Seconds passed that felt much longer. Finally, I asked again, "Did you eat the cookie, Ryder?" This time, he nodded, as tears welled up in his eyes.

I wasn't that hard on him. The only punishment he got was one less cookie when it was time for dessert. But it bothered him more than I thought it would. Evidently, when you're seven, the threat of only getting *one* after-dinner cookie—instead of the usual two—is quite disappointing and very unfair (even when a second cookie is already in your stomach). The sadness and anger swirled together on his face and made a new expression that seemed to say that *I* was the bad guy. "Don't talk to me," he declared from a place that appeared to come from a mixture of letdown and guilt. I let him go when he marched off to another room and announced in the process, "I'm not eating anything."

This time, my thoughts shifted to my Heavenly Father. "I've done this to You more times than I can remember, haven't I?" I asked God out loud rhetorically with a sheepish grin on my face, before continuing the spiritual dissection of my own behavior in my thoughts. *I do the sinning, and I either can't see it or don't want to admit it. Then, to add insult to the injury and hurt You even more, God, I stop talking to You. Maybe it's the shame. Maybe it's the feeling of defeat. Sometimes, it's the delusion of believing that You were actually the one at fault. In the end, it doesn't matter why. My sin has separated me from You, Abba.* **Again.**

This realization led me to seek out my own child that night. Between the guilt of getting caught and the disdain of being punished, I knew that he was unlikely to come to me and ask for forgiveness on his own anytime soon. And so, I pursued him—just as my Heavenly Father has pursued me. Over and over again, He has pursued me, and I've never deserved it. Call it mercy. Call it love. Call it things I don't even understand. All I know is that I'm so glad He's done it more times than I can count . . . and will *continue* to do it until the very end. He will do it for you, too.

CHAPTER EIGHTEEN

THE PRICE OF ONE OPPORTUNITY

"FOR GOD SO LOVED THE WORLD THAT HE GAVE HIS ONE AND ONLY SON, THAT WHOEVER BELIEVES IN HIM SHALL NOT PERISH BUT HAVE ETERNAL LIFE." JOHN 3:16 NIV

Although we had two cats in the family already—one for each of our daughters—Jason suggested that we adopt a third one for Ryder, our seven-year-old, fourth child who was still sleeping in our bed at night because it was "too lonely to be alone" in his own room. "How about a black kitten this time?" Jason proposed next, so that the new feline family member would be a different color than the others: Tigger, Meliah's orange Tabby, and Flash, Makenzie's gray and white tiger. I was on board and immediately set out to find Ryder's new best friend online, but it wouldn't prove to be as easy as it had been to find Tigger and Flash. Jason and Makenzie are allergic to cats, so we can only adopt Siberians, since they are hypoallergenic (to most people with a history of cat allergies). Thankfully, Siberians are in no way second-rate cats, as we have always found their reputation of being "the dogs of the cat world" to be fully true—ever since we adopted out first Siberian cat in 2002 before any of our children were born.

Tekha was flown to us in California from a breeder in Michigan, and, after the shockingly tiny calico kitten shook off her initial fears of us, she was amazingly friendly and bold. Clearly, she believed that she was our human child as much as any other could be. There was the usual cuddling, of course. But then there were the traits that are so unusual for most other cat breeds. She *loved* water—instead of hating it—and lived for the attack games Jason played with her! She didn't even try to hide her jealousy when our first child, Meliah, was born. Tekha died too young at the age of nine, but we have never forgotten the amazing personalities of the Siberian cat, which she had first introduced us to.

Adopting Tigger and Flash had also been easy. The same Texas breeder flew both kittens to us in Maryland just a month apart, and the entire process went off without a hitch.

So, I never imagined how difficult it would be to find a Siberian kitten for Ryder. Over and over again, I found websites whose breeders either told me that they didn't have any kittens at all or that they had a waiting list of buyers five times longer than the number of kittens they actually had to sell. Determined to bring a kitten home for my son before Christmas, I continued my search into the night the evening before Thanksgiving. Finally, I found a promising website.

Featured on the home page were photos of six adorable Siberian kittens—each of a different color with an accompanying description of their unique and charming personality. Already named, they appeared to be missing just one thing—their forever families. The breeders—who said they were registered with The International Cat Association (TICA)—were from a town in North Carolina that I had actually lived in for a few years. And their prices seemed reasonable. Better yet, the website indicated that the kitten could be sent right to your doorstep by a courier. I wouldn't even have to drive to the airport, as I had previously done to pick up Tekha, Tigger, and Flash.

Immediately, the kitten at the top of the page, Mike, caught my eye—for his fur was black. I emailed the breeder about my interest in Mike for my seven-year-old son, and she responded quickly with a video of a cute black kitten playing on a large treadmill wheel. The couple selling Mike had met and fallen in love in Russia, their website shared, while breeding Siberian kittens in their native country. I had known since 2002 that Siberians first came to the United States in 1990 after being traded to Russia for Himalayan cats from America. I noticed that the grammar from the website and emails wasn't perfect, but this didn't bother me, since I hadn't expected the English of Russian immigrants to be the same as that of native-born Americans.

The day after Thanksgiving, I signed the very detailed and professionally-appearing contract for Mike that had been provided to me—and paid the asking price of $1250. The excitement in my heart could hardly be contained as we put up our Christmas decorations that day, and I thought about how happy Ryder would be in just a couple of weeks when he held his very own kitten in his arms. I emailed a picture of Mike to my mother, whose love of cats surpasses that of most human beings on the planet, and she became excited, too. Only after dark did I rather suddenly realize the truth too late, as some oddities of the whole experience finally came to my awareness all at once—red flags I should have noticed much sooner along the way.

I scrolled through the information on the website again with my eyes wide open for the first time. Why did the breeder have so many ten-and eleven-week-old kittens of different colors available, and why weren't there any specific (and recent) birthdates listed? Why hadn't the breeder updated the website to show that any of the kittens had been sold? And why did the website's testimonials of even the American buyers contain the same imperfect grammar of the sellers? Worst of all, why had the seller, who wouldn't accept PayPal (as some sellers won't due to the fees attached) have Zelle and Cash App accounts in three different names—none of which matched the names of the breeders on the contract? When the Cash App transaction hadn't gone through, I had been provided with the contact information for the breeder's Zelle account, which was supposedly coming from their "business manager." Is that why I hadn't been bothered by the name discrepancies earlier in the day?

My heart felt sick. And although Jason is usually my best source of comfort in any disappointing situation, I didn't want to wake him up and have his sleep disturbed, too. Losing a large amount of money—that we actually needed to buy Christmas gifts for the entire family—was my fault, after all. Why should he have to suffer? I felt like an idiot, of course. *How could I have been so naive*? I asked myself over and over. I decided to email the breeder and tell "her" that I knew the truth, never expecting the denial that came next. The scammer wouldn't budge from his role as a Siberian kitten-selling, female immigrant from Russia. And that wasn't all. "She" told me that she felt bad that I thought she was a scammer, although she also understood. Undaunted, she told me that my son was going to have a big smile on his face in just a few days—and then maybe, my trust would also be restored.

Admittedly, I was perplexed. He *already* had my money, and I had no way to really find his true identity and location for the police—not to mention the fact that I'd be too embarrassed to call them anyway. So why not just admit everything at this point? Could this breeder actually be legitimate? Twenty-four hours passed without a reply to my last email, and once more, I was certain that I had been scammed. Then the following morning, I found a new email in my inbox. "Today's the day your kitten is coming!" it read, accompanied by a smiley-face emoji.

The motivation for the scammer's refusal to admit the truth at this point continued to elude me, since the fee for the courier had always been included in the original payment that I was sure had been stolen from me. "She" told me that she was just waiting for her ride to the courier company, and that she would message me later. But the day ended without another message . . . or a kitten. So, I sent my own message at ten o'clock. "My son isn't smiling like you promised." And then, for good measure, I added, "Why do you feel bad that I think you're a scammer, if that's what you really are?" Quickly, an apology came with an attempt to explain. "My ride came late and I forgot that the courier company closes early on Sundays."

The following day, I got a phone call at work. "Did you get our email?" a man with a thick accent that I couldn't place blurted out. "No," I replied. "We will be delivering your kitten tomorrow after five o'clock," he responded. "Read the email, and if everything is okay, you don't have to call back," I was instructed. For just a moment, a small part of me wondered if I had been too distrusting and skeptical. In contrast, the biggest part of me knew that I had just heard the voice of my scammer.

The email said that "Mikey" would be stopping at a station around midnight for a wellness check—and if needed, he would be given "pressure medicine." Of course, this would cost extra. But "if your kitten is strong and fit for transportation," there would be no additional fees. At the bottom of the email, there was a link for the website of the transportation company. It looked legitimate at first glance. The photography appeared professional and was pleasing to the eye.

But then the sleight of hand began to unravel. The web address itself was nearly identical to that of the transportation company it was masquerading as—except for one subtle change. It repeated portions of itself. Within the body of the website's text were grammatical errors that reminded me of the pretend breeder's, which I had once assumed were due to a second language barrier. There were obvious errors in the listed package weights as well. How could the combined weight of the carrier and kitten be less than the kitten himself?

The sting of the robbery had already been felt in the pit of my stomach three days earlier. I suddenly realized that it had since lost some of its power. Should I play along or tell the thief that his scam needed some work? I thought about it as I experienced a mixture of emotions, which still consisted of sadness and shame but now included amusement and a bit of unexpected pity as well. This dishonest crook couldn't possibly know Jesus—even if he'd heard about Him. Was I supposed to share my Savior with him now? I didn't know.

I began to ask myself questions about the man behind the scam. Does he have a real job? Does he need one? Does it really matter? How had he gotten to the point in his life where he could reassure the person he was robbing and lying to—even as he was still in the process of stabbing them in the back with a smiley-faced-emoji-covered knife? In his true light, he appeared far more callous than the average criminal. Even bank robbers, car jackers, and home invaders don't lie to you over and over and pretend that they're bringing you a gift.

As I was pondering these things, something happened in my heart. Defeated in the moment and resolved that I would be unable to change the outcome, I realized that I was still the lucky one. I could earn more money (the *right* way) and find another Siberian kitten. These things are replaceable. I could even get my pride back one day—or stop blaming myself instead. For although I don't want to be naive—or "a mark" or target, as my thief continuously reassured me that I wasn't—neither do I want to become so jaded or distrusting that I stop assuming most people are actually honest and decent. My luck had nothing to do with any of these things, however.

I knew that I was blessed, *not* because of my job or potential to buy the things I wanted, which is something that this con artist may have felt he didn't have. Instead, my greatest blessing is one that money can't buy and anyone can have—just for the asking. I wondered if my robber had ever been told that things could be better—regardless of his lot in life or the opportunities he may not have been given in this often unfair planet. Perhaps he had thrown away his opportunities instead because it seemed that he had found an easier way. In the end, it didn't matter. He was clearly missing the most important thing in my life, and I felt that I was supposed to give him something more valuable than the $1250 he had already taken from me.

So often in my life, I had thought that my forgiveness should be dependent on the remorse of the one who had hurt me, as if even God Himself didn't expect me to forgive someone who had never even asked. But now I knew differently. Though I was certain that this man would never admit he had wronged me—or even take me up on what I was about to offer—I felt that Jesus was asking me to do it anyways. "I forgive you," I wrote to him, without any strings attached. "Because of my best friend, Jesus—and only because of Him—I can forgive you. If you don't know Him, you are missing out on THE single greatest treasure of your life, and I feel sad for you, because you are missing the only thing that gets me through each day and gives me real peace. The money is ultimately worthless. Jesus would want me to share Him with you, if you are interested in knowing about Him and have ever wondered if there is actually more to this life than this."

He never acknowledged this email—or the mountain of evidence I had found that proved he had been lying. Instead, he continued to send me emails which said that my kitten would be arriving at my doorstep the following day, as long as he was still healthy enough to travel for the remaining portion of his journey without requiring the treatments that would cost an additional fee. "You will get a call around midnight with an update," he reminded me. Till the very end, my scammer never gave up. And from what I had been reading, the many victims of fake online pet adoptions often lose more money during the second half of the scam than they do in the beginning. Where there is money and naivety, there must be more, after all.

Finally, I said goodbye. "I won't be worried about a kitten who doesn't exist," I told the man who had once tricked me. These words were for *me*. My last words, however, were for him instead. "There really is a God who loves you, but if you continue doing what you're doing and don't get to know Him, there will be a reckoning one day. If you want to know more about God and His son Jesus, I really would be happy to share. Otherwise, please do not contact me again." (In full disclosure, the last sentence may not have actually contained the word please, and the word "not" after it might have been put in capital letters—I'm definitely not perfect.)

Time has taken away the emotions that I felt that night I first realized I'd been lied to and stolen from. Only the memory is there at this point, and I don't even think of it most days. Ryder has a *real* Siberian kitten now—a white one named Hurricane—and life has moved on. I'd like to say that my scammer took me up on my offer to share with him the "score" of an *eternal* lifetime, but he didn't. I've realized, however, that if I'd never been robbed by this man, he might never even have been given the chance. Just t he *opportunity* he was given cost me a lot, and I had never consented to pay for it.

But someone did exactly that for you and me. Very intentionally, Jesus chose to pay an infinitely greater price simply to give us a chance for salvation, all the while knowing that like my scammer, most will never accept it. And His Father gave up His most valued treasure, the Son He loves more than Himself. Our opportunity to choose salvation cost Him everything, too—even if we don't take advantage of it. Both of them were willing to pay the infinite price and experience the indescribable suffering that it required.

So, say **yes** to the incredible gift we've been given. Never let the cost of this precious opportunity go to waste. Say **yes** to the Hearts of mercy who are hoping that their sacrifice won't be for nothing (but who would do it all over again anyway).

CHAPTER NINETEEN

JUST FOR THE ASKING

"DELIGHT YOURSELF ALSO IN THE LORD, AND HE SHALL GIVE YOU THE DESIRES OF YOUR HEART."
PSALMS 37:4 NKJV

Sometimes God says no—to small things and big things. I know that from personal experience. Most of those times, I have eventually seen His wisdom and thanked Him for those very nos. But sometimes, He says yes—to big things and small things—just because I asked and believed. This story is about one of those experiences. Jesus called God "Abba, Father," so I do too, because the title "Abba" reflects His relationship to me so much better than plain old "God" does—not that there is anything plain or generic about my God. I respect my Heavenly Father immensely and indescribably, and I never want to presume that He'll say yes—or treat Him like a magic genie lamp. So, I often pray that I will also have a humble spirit, and as I relive this incredible story, I pray it again even now.

It was finally time for Ryder's much anticipated—and already loved—Siberian kitten to come home to Maryland from his first home in McAllen, Texas. Located at the very bottom of the state of Texas, the city of McAllen nearly borders Mexico. And it gets *hot*. Though it was only April, a high of 97 degrees was predicted in McAllen for the day of Hurricane Glacier's big flight. Even at 12:06 p.m.—the time that his plane was scheduled to take off—it was already supposed to be 84 degrees. And this mattered very much to us because the only airline left who was still willing to transport unaccompanied pets during the pandemic had a strict policy regarding temperatures: No flying animals outside of the acceptable temperature range—44 to 85 degrees—at *any* point in their journey, from beginning to end.

Our breeder Nathan and I both watched the hour-by-hour weather forecast intently for twenty-four hours. At one point, the predicted temperature for McAllen, Texas on the date planned for Hurricane's flight was going to be exactly 84 degrees at noon. Not once did it fall below 84 degrees, and the predicted temperature at one o'clock was 86 degrees–*too high*. Any delay of the flight or slight increase in the temperature would result in Hurricane being sent back home. Such a scenario had happened to Nathan and the kittens of other adoptive families before. American Airlines meant business.

The prospects for our back-up plan weren't much better. There were no cargo flights for unaccompanied pets on Saturdays or Sundays. And the following Friday afternoon—the next best time for Jason to pick Hurricane up from the airport—was predicted to be just as hot. His flight could potentially even be delayed twice. I tried to prepare my eight-year-old for these possibilities so that he wouldn't be as disappointed if they actually happened. But I knew that it would be a crushing blow to my child just the same. Already, he had waited three weeks since unwrapping his surprise birthday present and finding the personalized, yellow kitten collar and photo of his new baby within a gold, cat-shaped picture frame. And when you're eight, every day that you can't put your arms around your new furry friend undoubtedly feels like a year.

It seemed like a good time to pray. Jason and I prayed. Nathan and his wife and young daughter prayed. Even my mother prayed. And little Ryder prayed, too. I had taken a chance and advised him to do it—knowing full well that if God's answer was no, my child would take that to heart. It wasn't an easy decision, considering the obvious fact that my young child's developing faith could be tested. But I decided to trust my Heavenly Father enough to risk it. After all, why should I worry about a potential problem that involves the weather? My Abba is in charge of the weather. I thought about the times that I had neglected to ask for His help with various problems of mine and how many days or months I'd wasted. When I finally asked Him to intervene, He had done so remarkably quickly, and I could hear Him whispering to my heart, "What took you so long? I thought you'd never ask."

So, I laid all of our hopes and fears at my Abba's feet. Ryder and I both prayed for the temperature not to rise even a single degree above the airline's 85 degree cut off in McAllen, Texas, at exactly noon on the day of little Hurricane's big flight home. For twenty-four hours—no matter how many times I looked at the forecast—the predicted temperature never budged from 84 degrees at noon and 86 degrees at one o'clock. And the predicted chance of rain? *Zero* percent. No chance at all.

The following morning when I woke up, I immediately got down on my knees by my bed and prayed the exact same prayer. Ryder woke up about fifteen minutes later—far earlier than he was supposed to—because he was just too excited and nervous to sleep. As I was got ready for work, my eight-year-old asked me, "Should we do it again?" At first, I had no idea what he was talking about. "Do what again, Angel Boy?" I asked him to explain. "Pray," he answered simply. This mother's reply was a no brainer. "Yes, Honey. We should do it again."

I checked my phone between each patient's visit at work and watched the temperature rise higher and higher. Still no rain in the forecast, either. Finally, I decided to ask God very specifically for rain because I knew that rain would cool the airport down. And once I had prayed for rain, I didn't have time to check the weather app again, as things got busier and busier at work. The outcome was in God's hands now, and although I still didn't know how the story would end, the feeling of stress that so often accompanies uncertainty simply melted away.

Then just one hour before the scheduled take-off, I got another text from Nathan. "They accepted him! Little Glacier is on his way. It started to rain. It was like a mist at first, and I think it cooled things down. I even had to use my windshield wipers on the way home." I quickly looked at the weather app again. The predicted temperatures for noon and one o'clock—which hadn't budged in twenty-four hours—had suddenly dropped by three degrees. Now the mist was in my eyes, and I could see my Abba wink at me in my mind.

The God of the Universe is very real, and He is still actively involved in the lives of those who love and (try to) obey Him—just as He was in Bible times. This story depicts only one of the many times when the God of Heaven bent down and listened to my heart with His own. To this world, I am nothing special. The list of things I *don't* have is undoubtedly longer than the list of things that I do. No fame or social media following. No great wealth or power. Not even a long list of souls I have won for the Kingdom of Heaven that the Christian world can admire.

So why has God said yes to so many of my prayer requests? I suspect that there are multiple reasons—just as there have been numerous reasons why He has also had to say no to many of my seemingly good plans and desires. The biggest reason, however, is that He simply cannot help Himself. He's a Father who wants to give good gifts to His much loved children—especially when they trust Him. Beyond that, I think that God has done these incredible things for me because He knew that I would write about them and share these stories with *you*.

CHAPTER TWENTY

TRUST OR SIN

"YOU WILL KEEP IN PERFECT PEACE ALL WHO TRUST IN YOU, ALL WHOSE THOUGHTS ARE FIXED ON YOU! TRUST IN THE LORD ALWAYS, FOR THE LORD GOD IS THE ETERNAL ROCK." ISAIAH 26:3-4 NLT

His comment took me by surprise. As I was complimenting my patient for his perfect blood pressure and lab results, which signified that his hypertension, diabetes, and high cholesterol were well-controlled, I also told him that I could see that he was taking his prescribed medications. Matter-of-factly, he had replied, "You're the doctor. You told me to take them, so I did." Now he was the one who was surprised. "Doesn't everybody do that?" he innocently asked. "Oh no," I told him. "There are plenty of patients who don't take their medications or follow my advice. That's why I must give credit where credit is due—to *you*."

The words he spoke next have stuck with me. "I didn't go to medical school. You did. And I trust you." There are too many spiritual lessons that find me in my day-to-day life to even count, and I knew that this would be one of them. I thought about the origin of sin, both in Heaven with Lucifer and with Eve—and then Adam—in the Garden of Eden. Sure, there was

Hubris in each case—the word for pride that I had learned in my college Greek literature course, which refers specifically to the kind of pride that leads one to arrogantly believe they are like the "gods." But Hubris—or the pride of delusion—ultimately comes from the lack of something else that is the most critical safeguard against sin—trust. That's not to say that humility isn't important and protective against sin in its own right. But even humility would not have been enough to keep sin from entering our world if trust was missing.

I realized that even my patient didn't trust me *solely* because I'm a physician. Human physicians can be wrong, of course, and I am certain he was aware of that. As the years have passed—and I have practiced medicine for longer—I have come to understand that even patients who come to me with pre-existing fears about a particular medication or treatment will often agree to take it if they have known me long enough to discover personally that I am trustworthy and have their best interest at heart. They don't have to know everything that I know—although I enjoy educating my patients so that they, too, feel good about doing what I've advised. Ultimately, unless they can become me—and live inside my brain—they will need to trust me if I am going to have any chance of healing them or keeping them well.

Unlike me and my fellow human physicians, God will never steer you wrong. But do you truly believe that? Have you spent enough time with Him to develop the kind of trust that's needed to obey Him? What if Lucifer had trusted God more than his own ideas of fairness and freedom? What if Eve had trusted that God would never keep something from her that would actually have allowed her to be her best self or experience true joy? What if Adam had trusted God to find the perfect solution for the devastation he felt when he realized that his beloved wife had been deceived by the enemy?

Trust in God is our best defense against sin—at least, that's what I've found to be true in my own life. Will I always understand why God says no or asks me to do something that I don't want to? Of course not, for I am not God. But I trust Him. On my best days, that's enough to keep me from sinning—though my righteousness is still like filthy rags. On my worst days, I hurt God by trusting my limited knowledge more than the wisdom of the One who created me.

Trust God or sin. Though she didn't understand it yet, this was the decision that both God and Lucifer had set before Eve at the tree. It's the same decision that Adam was faced with just a short time later. And it is still the choice that we are given each and every day, even now. Thankfully, we aren't left without an example. God's own Son showed us how to trust His Father in the worst possible situation—when His very life was at stake, and the suffering was almost more than He could bear. If Jesus can trust God, then we can too.

It won't simply be our recreation at the resurrection that keeps us from sinning in Heaven. Neither will it be our increased knowledge that prevents us from being misled all over again. For we will always have the freedom to question God, and we will never know as much as He does. Hindsight and its memories of the horrors of sin will always be an important safeguard against the return of the pride that led to evil in the first place. But I believe that the protection this brings on its own will also be surprisingly inadequate.

There is only one thing that will keep sin out of the Kingdom of Heaven forever: trust in the Father & Son. And even this ability is a gift that we are given through the remembrance of just one day in history. When we are finally living the lives that we were meant to live from the beginning, and Satan is no longer able to hurt us—or cause us to hurt each other—we will still remember the staggering cost of our freedom. And as our fingers find their way into the nail scarred hands of our Redeemer throughout eternity, the trust that we need to keep from sinning will flood our hearts and minds over and over again.

CHAPTER TWENTY-ONE

STICK WITH HIM

"TURN TO ME AND BE SAVED, ALL YOU ENDS OF THE EARTH; FOR I AM GOD, AND THERE IS NO OTHER." ISAIAH 45:22 NIV

The snow was beautiful to me. It always has been. Even as a child, growing up in the suburbs of Boston, I had marveled at the fact that giant piles of white, breathtaking fun could be made from tiny ice flakes. It saddened me when these glistening mounds of snow either melted away or became marred by the dirty tires of passing cars, after they had been shoveled from the road and pushed up against the city curbs. In Massachusetts, the next winter snow was never far away, but in Maryland where I live in now, the next snow of the season is never guaranteed.

As the days passed and the temperatures rose, the snow melted—just as the laws of nature command it to do. "Until we meet again," I whispered out loud in my car, as if the storehouses of snow could actually hear me. Another week went by, with daytime high temperatures well above freezing. I noticed a giant hill of snow in the corner of my work building's parking lot and wondered how it had survived the temperatures in the mid-40s. Several more days passed, and the temperature climbed above

50 degrees. Still, the lone mound of snow continued to exist, seemingly resistant to the heat that was supposed to destroy it.

When the temperature was nearly 60 degrees, and the large wall of snow continued to withstand the morning sun, I knew there was a lesson here for all of us. All of the smaller piles of snow that had been alone were long gone. From ice crystals to water and from water to air they had transitioned until they were no more. By themselves, they were powerless to prevent their demise—no match for the laws of nature that ultimately marked them for evaporation.

In my imagination, the mini-mountain of snow became a lifelike being, just as a snowman had once become Frosty in the famous 1969 movie we so often sing about at Christmas time.[1] The parking lot mountain was now personified and warned me of our own fate that lies ahead. "Stand alone, and the heat will beat you. There is only one way to stay alive. Stick with the One who can fight death for you, and you can live forever."

Of course, I knew that there was a science equation behind the strange phenomenon I had observed day after day. The larger the volume of snow, the longer it would take to melt, even at a higher temperature. But I still couldn't miss the spiritual lesson that nature appeared to be displaying for me. The law of sin and death has reigned over every living being since Adam. There is no way to hide from it. No way to escape. No probability at all—however small—that we can defeat this terrible enemy.

Even worse, we don't actually deserve to win. And let's face it, we aren't "safe to save" yet either, to use the three words from one of my favorite authors, Graham Maxwell, that have always made so much sense to me.[2] Think about what harm we would cause to the angels of Heaven (and continue to do to each other) if we were admitted to the Kingdom in our current, sinful state. Sounds pretty hopeless, huh? That's because it actually is. But our stories don't have to end this way, and that declaration isn't a fantasy.

The truth is far better than the greatest movie you've ever watched. The bad guy has already been defeated by the good guy, but not in the way that anyone imagined. He secured His future victory by *dying*. And unlike the rest of us, Death required His consent to take His life. The good guy in our story was filled with more than an altruistic desire to save the world from evil—although that's certainly something He wanted. His primary motivation was one that none of the greatest super heroes of Hollywood's creation have ever had: **love**.

It's our Hero's love that saved us, and this Savior's love that changes our sinful hearts and makes us "safe to save."[3] In the movies, none of the characters know which leader is going to win. Would they choose a different master if they did? Perhaps.... But we know who has already won this war that we've all become pawns in. Let's not allow the one who cares nothing about us to take us as prisoners of war, simply because we aren't clinging to the only One who can free us from that inevitable destiny.

Stick with Jesus, like the tiny ice crystals that stick together and become such beautiful mounds of pure white snow. Cling to the Hero of the "Backwards Kingdom"[4] whose humility led to our salvation. Stick with Him. There is no reason that you have to melt away. "For why will you die?" (excerpt from Ezekiel 33:11 English Standard Version)

Chapter Twenty-Two

A TALE OF TWO HEARTS

"TODAY I HAVE GIVEN YOU THE CHOICE BETWEEN LIFE AND DEATH, BETWEEN BLESSINGS AND CURSES. NOW I CALL ON HEAVEN AND EARTH TO WITNESS THE CHOICE YOU MAKE. OH, THAT YOU WOULD CHOOSE LIFE, SO THAT YOU AND YOUR DESCENDANTS MIGHT LIVE!"
DEUTERONOMY 30:19 NLT

O nce upon a time, there were two men in need of new hearts. Without this priceless gift, death was imminent for each of them. Yes, medications had bought them time—but ultimately, the drugs would not be strong enough to save them. They needed healthy heart muscle to pump their life's blood to the rest of the organs in their failing bodies. So, they stood in line on "the transplant list," a seemingly impersonal, computerized record of names representing thousands of real-world souls in need o f *living* replacements for their weak and damaged hearts. No biotech company—however talented in the ways of modern technology—could ever truly copy the design of the Creator.

The priority ranking of the two men moved up and down the list as their conditions worsened and improved, worsened and improved, and then worsened and improved all over again—until finally, there was no more improvement to be had at all. The hospital became their home. Their heart medications would be given as long as their blood pressure was at least 70 systolic each half-day, because the beta-blocker and ACE-inhibitor were their Lifeguards. Hypotension and dizziness were still preferable to death, after all.

As their failing literal hearts struggled to keep up with the needs of the body, their figurative hearts wrestled with the same questions that they didn't actually want to ask. *What if I die before a new heart comes?* the men wondered during the long and lonely days that were filled with pills, blood pressure checks, daily weights, and beeping monitors. And as they tried to find a comfortable position to sleep in each night—with all of the attached lines and tubes—they couldn't help but ask themselves silently, *Will I even wake up tomorrow?* How strange it felt to wish for a new heart, knowing full well that in order for this to happen, someone else must suffer the worst possible fate.

The call of a (*second*) lifetime came for each of them the same year. Their lives would be saved, because someone else had died and provided something they needed for survival but could never buy. For each human soul, it was their do-over of grace. So, the weak, enlarged, and flabby hearts were removed—and in their place, each man received a new heart made of strong, healthy cardiac muscle. Medications were started to prevent their immune systems from rejecting the "foreign" tissue of their donors, and life outside the hospital was actually possible once again. How grateful they were! It's easy to feel that way when you've been given a coveted gift that could've easily been given to someone else. Even winning a billion-dollar lottery could never compare, for what good is having everything that money can buy if you aren't going to be alive to enjoy it?

Now this is the part of the story where I come in, for each man walked into my exam room about two years after they had walked out of the hospital, with their new hearts beating powerfully and dependably inside their once diseased chests. Listening to their hearts with my stethoscope was an amazing privilege that never got old. How quickly the transplanted heart beats without the usual attachment to the vagus nerve that normally slows the heart rate of a congenital or natural-born heart.

Remarkably, four years into my relationship with these heart transplant recipients, they contracted the exact same infection within a month of each other. Both men were hospitalized—but only one of them came home. And for the one who didn't, even the most valiant efforts of physicians with all of modern medicine at their disposal simply weren't powerful enough to save him. Once again, a priceless heart stopped beating inside his chest.

I cannot help but see the spiritual parallels for all of us. We, too, are in critical need of new hearts, for the ones we were born with are killing us, slowly but surely. Incredibly, a Man with a perfect heart consented to death, because He knew that it was the only way to share His heart with us and save our lives. The realities of this plan of salvation are far better than that of any earthly transplant program, for there is no shortage of new organs. *All* who want to live will be granted new hearts, if only they are willing to cling to the One who wants to heal them.

I can only imagine that the angels in Heaven once assumed that we would all accept this incredible and undeserved offer. How shocked they must have been when the truth became apparent. Far more of us prefer independence and death over obedience and life, although we rarely see things in this light. For the enemy of our would-be Savior has been lying from the very beginning—telling the angels even before us that God's commandments were robbing them of their freedom, when the truth was exactly the opposite.[1] Oh, the misery that this supposed freedom has brought back upon our own heads! Disappointment and hurt. A ball and chain around our ankles. Pain and suffering that is sometimes too ugly to speak out loud—even and *especially* against the most innocent.

Will we gratefully and enthusiastically take the new heart that Jesus died to purchase for us and then go on to live a different life in order to preserve it? Will we, instead, refuse to be healed altogether, preferring to be sick because we believe that it will be easier and better somehow? Or, will we try to split the difference, taking the new heart because we don't want to die, yet still going back to our old lives—the very lives that allowed the hearts we were born with to become damaged in the first place? The decision is ours

.

That is the freedom we have always been given—to choose life and wellness by following the advice of our Creator, or to choose the death and destruction that will inevitably result from following the ways that seem right to us instead. There is a deceiver who wants to trick and harm you. At best, he cares nothing about you. At worst, he wants to rob you of life for eternity. Listen to the One who forever settled the question as to whether or not He is trustworthy by laying down His own life.

This Heavenly doctor wants to be *our* personal physician, and unlike the ones my patients had received, the heart transplant He offers us is everlasting. Of course, our sinful nature causes us to reject it, just as the human body naturally rejects the lifesaving heart of another man unless anti-rejection medications are taken with it daily forever. Yet hope is not lost. This same Jesus who died to give us a new heart can also draw us to His own, over and over again. Why He would want to fight for this wandering spirit of mine is something I will never completely understand, but I'm so thankful that He does. "Don't give up on me," I've whispered to my

Savior, more times than I can count. And each time, He speaks plainly to my sin-sick heart, "Not a chance."

CHAPTER TWENTY-THREE

THE PILOT

"LET THE MORNING BRING ME WORD OF YOUR UNFAILING LOVE, FOR I HAVE PUT MY TRUST IN YOU. SHOW ME THE WAY I SHOULD GO, FOR TO YOU I ENTRUST MY LIFE." PSALMS 143:8 NIV

The first time I flew in a commercial airplane, I wasn't even old enough to go to school. Not only was I too innocent to realize that the plane could crash with *me* inside of it, I didn't even know that death existed yet. From Massachusetts to California and Disneyland I went, in just half a day's journey—and from that point on, I decided that I loved flying. As I grew older, I realized that it wasn't only the plane and the view from the window seat that excited me, it was the airport itself. I loved everything about it: the hustle and bustle of fellow travelers headed to their various destinations for mysterious reasons; shops filled with souvenirs, magazines, and snacks; restaurants and coffee shops. I enjoyed long layovers and tried to get to the airport as early as possible, so that I could spend even more time in my happy place before my flight's scheduled departure.

Of course, this enamoration with all things airlines would never be possible without one thing: trust in the pilot. We trust a lot of layers in a process that is designed to keep us safe. We trust that the Federal Aviation

Administration will require adequate training in order for a pilot's license to be granted—and then we trust that the companies who interview each candidate will actually verify that this license is valid. But ultimately, we trust the pilot most. We trust that he wasn't satisfied to learn just the minimum during his years of training. We trust that she didn't come to work under the influence of alcohol or drugs today. Though we rarely see him, we trust the pilot. We walk onto the plane, sit in our seats—and even *relax*—because we trust the pilot.

Never have I been more aware of my blind trust in pilots than I was on the day that I actually met one face-to-face in my clinic. He was wearing his street clothes, as most of my patients do. I took his medical and social history and quickly discovered that we have some things in common. Like me, he is married with children—a fellow human being in his forties who was in need of some preventative health care of his own. But that's where the similarities stopped. I learned that he is a professional pilot—and not just any pilot, I might add. It turns out that he flies for my favorite airline! Silently, I wondered if he had ever been the pilot for one of *my* flights.

As I thought about the humanness of the pilots that we trust so easily, I couldn't help but wonder why it's so difficult for us to trust the God who actually made us. How often do we think we know what's best for us and become frustrated with Him—*or worse*—when He says no or makes us wait? How many times have we blamed God for the bad things that happen to us because we think that He should've have prevented them—if He really is good and truly loves us? While I will never pretend to have the all of the answers to the great and very personal questions about suffering, I believe that I've at least figured out why we trust the earthly pilot. He (almost) always takes us to the destination that we've requested. It's easy to trust a pilot when she has a record of doing exactly what we've asked.

What if we took a moment to acknowledge that we wouldn't even be able to form an opinion about God's decisions if He hadn't created us with the brain power to analyze His behavior in the first place? That has got to count for something. The God who says, "Come now, and let us reason together," in Isaiah 1:18 (KJV) doesn't actually want us to get on His plane blindly. He craves our trust even more than He desires our willingness to simply follow His plan. Playing follow-the-leader is something that any lemming or sheep can do, after all.

Perhaps the best pilot isn't actually the one who will consistently take us wherever we ask. Maybe the pilot we truly need is the one who will fly us away from the trouble that we can't see or take us to a place that's better than the one we had originally requested—even if that destination comes by way of a longer journey. I may have good ideas about where the plane should take me, but it doesn't change the fact that **I am not a pilot**. I can't see the sky in front of me just behind the fog any more than I can see the distant horizon far beyond my own lens' depth of field, for **I am not a pilot**. *Are you?*

There is a Heavenly Pilot who is far more experienced than the human pilots we routinely trust with our lives without a moment's hesitation—a Pilot who hasn't just seen the entirety of the skies but actually created them. He is better than the pilot who is merely able to follow directions. He is worth more than a pilot who is merely too skilled to crash. The Pilot who wants to fly you is smarter, more experienced, and even able to see the future. But these aren't the factors that make Him most trustworthy. This Pilot **knows you**, inside and out. He **loves you** and was willing to trade His life for yours. It really doesn't get any better than that.

CHAPTER TWENTY-FOUR

RESTORATION

"HE RESTORES MY SOUL. HE LEADS ME IN PATHS OF RIGHTEOUSNESS FOR HIS NAME'S SAKE."
PSALMS 23:3 NKJV

M y eyes were drawn to it immediately, as I passed by the single-item yard sale on my way to work. A sight for sore eyes, it was *not*. Rather, sore eyes the sight of it inflicted. My brain instinctively told me that it was a convertible vehicle from the late 1950s or early 1960s—just as it tells me that I am looking at a deceased human being when I see skeletal remains—but that was about all I could imagine. No paint remained—none at all—unless you consider rust to be the paint of nature. Then, there were the dents.... To me, it just appeared to be a hunk of junk in need of a tow truck. Instead, there was a giant For Sale sign attached to it.

The intent to sell this dilapidated piece of metal on wheels (which I would later learn is a 1964 Chevrolet) told me that its owner assumed that it would be valuable to *someone*—even if my eyes couldn't see its worth. From my vantage point, the dream seemed far-fetched. Not only was the object in front of me undoubtedly ugly, I assumed that it would cost more to restore the car than it would ultimately be worth in its refurbished state. Clearly, the seller knew this too, and that's why they were trying to unload it. Or perhaps, they simply couldn't afford to pay for the rehab. Either way, I thought it was a money pit.

Around this same time, I discovered that in his retirement, my father has grown to love reality television shows featuring car restorations on the Motor Trend channel. One morning, on our joint vacation, I watched along with him—just to keep him company. And I saw the most unexpected and *amazing* transformations of a 1957 Ford Wagon, a 1973 Mustang, and even a 1934 Dodge that had been in the same family for eighty years. From frames of scrap metal hardly recognizable as vehicles to shiny, beautiful automobiles, they were transformed. The metamorphosis happened under the hoods as well. In each reconstruction, the dead parts of the vehicle were replaced with new ones that gave life to the car once again.

The parallels to my own state of being simply could not be ignored. As much as I like to fancy myself as something akin to a gorgeous remodeled car from the *Hand Built Hot Rods* show,[1] the reality is that I'm more like the decaying piece of rusted metal that I now drive by daily on my way to work. Even on the good days, my appearance is a far cry from that of the first woman God created, and my insides are too often dead in the eyes of Heaven. My best behavior is no better because my "righteousness is like filthy rags" (Isaiah 64:6 NKJV).

Unfortunately for me and everyone I come in contact with, I can't afford the cost of my much-needed transformation either. And even if I could, there is no one on earth who is capable of completing the renovation—not even *Pure Vision Design*'s Steve Strope.[2] Like the law of entropy that causes once perfect red barns to morph into dilapidated shells of rotting, gray wood, my physical and moral decay cannot be stopped. There is no investor who can look past my flawed façade and see what I might become. The ending to my story is inevitable—unless someone intervenes.

I wondered who could find me worthy enough to redeem. And then, as if on cue—just two seconds after I drove past that rusty old convertible—I heard the answer to my question on the radio. "God, You restore,"[3] the song declared, and I knew that it was true. "Restoration we declare in Jesus." Only He could do what needed to be done in order to salvage the wreckage that sin has made of us. Only He had enough love to pay the exorbitant cost that our recreation requires. Without Him, we have no hope. With Him, we have *every* hope.

There is no in between. No partial transformation. No half restoration. No discounted DYI or do-it-yourself renovation. Our rescue from the scrap metal yard will require a loving Savior with genius and heart. It'll take a gracious Restorer with unlimited resources and perfect skill.

Left to our own devices, we could never hope to find this ultimate Deliverer. Thankfully, we don't have to. If you have been waiting to be made new, you don't have to wait anymore. There is a faithful Redeemer who wants to heal you from the inside out. And though the cost of your restoration is far greater than your apparent worth, He declares you to be priceless.

CHAPTER TWENTY-FIVE

EXPIRED

"PRECIOUS IN THE SIGHT OF THE LORD IS THE DEATH OF HIS SAINTS." PSALMS 116:15 NKJV

D octoring fellow human beings is truly the most amazing privilege. Every pre-med college student, medical student, intern, and resident is counting on this to be true, as they work harder and give up more personal time and hours of sleep than you could ever imagine. They hope that all of their sacrifice will be worth it in the end. And then, when they finally become "the attending physician," they discover that the job comes with pluses and minuses—just like any other profession. There will be good days and bad days when they least expect them.

On the bad days, there are frustrations with bureaucracies that haven't actually been in the trenches they make policies about. There are patients who wish that you could do more for them than you are able to—and patients who don't get well because they won't (or can't) follow your advice. There are days when you don't have the answer—or wish yourself that you had made different decisions. There is *endless* paperwork. And there are more phone and patient portal messages than you have hours in the day to respond to, so you come home later to your family in the evenings than you feel good about.

On the good days, there are interesting mysteries that ultimately lead to unique discoveries. Your advice is spot-on, and the ears are receptive to it. There are moments of healing and opportunities to encourage. The schedule leaves room for real conversations with patients. Long-term relationships of trust—and even familial love—develop. You can't believe how lucky you are to be able to make a living this way—until you realize that you've actually been *blessed* instead.

The one aspect of doctoring that's always been part of the deal—the piece that could never be placed in any category—is death. In the years since I first became a physician, I've tried to protect my patients from Death as long as I could, but he refuses to be cheated completely. Some of his victims were pronounced by me in the hospital after lengthy middle-of-the-night "codes" or resuscitation efforts in residency training. Other lives Death claimed without me being present, and I was only notified of his victory later by phone. Oh, how I have hated these calls—both those that were expected and those that were not!

"Expired," they've said to me too many times to count, as if such a euphemism could ever take the sting of Death away. I still know that an irreplaceable, one-of-a-kind human being has been lost—not merely a carton of souring milk. "Expired," they report, in order to sound more clinical, because the words died and passed away aren't in the medical dictionary, and we must always be professional and proper whenever we are documenting something in the patient's chart. Life itself has a shelf life, they imply, although it was never meant to be that way.

The length of time that I have known my patients before their supposed "expiration" has varied widely. I've lost patients I had never even met, who were already in a coma when I became their physician in the intensive care unit. I've also lost patients that I had known so long—and become so close to—that I considered them to be family. For most of them, it fell to me to complete their death certificate. And I have considered it to be a solemn responsibility and privilege each and every time. Few things in life so bitter can actually be called an honor—and very unexpectedly— this has been one of them. As the strokes of my pen make contact with the thick parchment paper, I cannot help but reminisce about the moments we spent together. Sometimes, I even imagine the moment that my patients' birth certificates were filled out decades earlier by parents so full of hope and excitement—most of whom have long since passed away themselves.

"You were here," I whisper out loud for each one of them as I say good-bye, alone at my desk. In order for you to understand the significance of these words, I must first explain their origin. Years ago, I watched a movie in which a man was dying at home and had no one with him in the final moments of his life, other than a nurse or physician who was present simply because it was their job. The man regretted that he had spent his life in isolation—working hard but making no real effort to develop any true, personal relationships. He shared his deepest fear with the stranger attending his death—that there would be no one to even remember that he was ever here on this earth. Although I cannot remember the name of the movie, there is one thing I have never forgotten. After the man dies—in defiance of his greatest fear—the empathetic hospice nurse or physician quickly says out loud, "You were here. You were here...."

At least those are the words that have somehow etched themselves into my memory. When my *days* long search for the movie's title via every possible avenue on the internet proved to be in vain (of which Google, movie quote searches and descriptions via IMDb, Facebook and the 1. 3-million-member "What is my movie?" subgroup on Reddit were only a few), my daughter Meliah suggested to me that I had simply imagined these particular words. Perhaps. For I cannot remember the face of either actor during that final death scene either. Neither do I recall the gender or job title of the only human being to witness this hopeless man take his final breath. Most strangely to me as a physician, I cannot even remember the specific disease that was killing him. Surely, Dr. Martz would at least remember that!

As I racked my brain in its fruitless attempt to remember something more, I began to realize something important—even if it's not "the important" that I thought I was searching for. Maybe the most poignant part of the movie isn't any of the things that I nearly wanted to pull my hair out for not remembering as I was writing this chapter of the book. If you are reading this book and wrote that scene from my mystery movie, then please let me know so that I can thank you for the impact you have had. But if that never happens, then let me learn something else from the frustration over my forgetfulness.

This haziness, too, provides a lesson for all of us. Just as the man dying with only the companionship of a hospice professional fears that his entire life is about to amount to nothing—and the entire script of a movie boils down to the sliver of a single scene—so it is that none of the rest of the details of our own lives will matter or be remembered when it's time for us to go. It won't matter how many friends we have collected or what we did to make a living. Neither will it matter what is listed as the specific cause of our demise on that parchment paper that bears our name. None of the things that surround the final scene of our life will be important when that time comes for us.

Death takes his victims without emotion—or even breaking a sweat—because he knows that his victory is certain in every battle. "For the living know that they will die..." (excerpt from Eccl. 9:5) We've known it for as long as we can remember. While I can't recall the exact moment that I learned about death in my own early childhood, God does. And I believe that He experienced a moment of sadness as He watched each of us discover this horrible reality for the first time. From that point on, there has been an unspoken fear of this beast called Death. Whether we acknowledge it out loud or simply admit it to ourselves silently, we routinely live in fear of this enemy. And even if we choose not to worry about the possibility of our own untimely death, we still worry about losing the ones that we love. We may not think about it every day. We may not even think about it for very long on *any* day (for if we did, it would be too difficult to get through this life). But still, we think about it.

Jesus knew that we would think about it, too. Long before we knew that we would need it, He and His Father came up with a plan to save us from *expiration*. This plan can be described in many ways: astonishing, jaw dropping, mind-boggling, risky, daring, chivalrous, heroic, costly, and exorbitant. But no adjective or combination of adjectives can adequately describe it because none of them could ever take into account the only thing that made this incomprehensible sacrifice worth it to our Savior in the first place—**love**.

Forty years into this mortal life of mine, I finally discovered the verse in the Bible that would immediately and permanently become my favorite: "Inasmuch then, as the children have partaken of flesh and blood, He Himself likewise shared in the same, that through death He might destroy him who had the power of death, that is, the devil, and release those who through fear of death were all their lifetime subject to slavery" (Hebrews 2:14-15 NKJV). It melted my heart the very first time I read it, and it has changed *everything*. Of course, I already knew that Jesus had died to save me. But the inclusion of this verse in the book that He inspired told me something more. Our Maker knew that the Death He was fighting on our behalf is more than just an end for us.

Jesus knew that the very knowledge of it leads to a fear-infused life that ultimately robs us of our freedom and darkens even the short period of time that we actually do get to live. Our empathetic Savior didn't simply want to destroy Death for us. He also wanted to free us from the anticipation of it. Can you imagine a world without the constant stream of death notices that we're exposed to daily? Some are personal—heartbreakingly personal. And the rest—which bombard us from the many news networks and social media sites—still serve to remind us that *none* of us are safe. The good die along with the bad. The young die along with the old. The healthy die along with the sick.

There are no guarantees of immunity from death for any of us—for even short periods of time. The only certainty in this life is that Death will come for us all. We can sometimes delay Death, but we can never defeat him. There is only one Champion who can do that. And He *did*. Satan can't change the outcome of the war anymore, although he desperately wants to and is still inflicting casualties even now. Our Rescuer has already secured the victory. We simply need to stay by His side until the very end.

For years, I have echoed the message that I admired about a movie I cannot even remember. *Finally*, I understand that having been here on this earth just isn't enough. It's not enough for me, and it's not enough for the patients I've cared about. Yes, their lives mattered. They mattered to me even if there is no one else to remember them. But I want more. I *need* more. And Jesus knew this even before I did. There's an epilogue that we will all crave deeply when the end of our own stories come. Thank God that He and His Son made a way for this to happen. It will forever melt my heart that my Redeemer laid down His life to extend mine.

CHAPTER TWENTY-SIX

TRANSMISSION

"I AM THE VINE; YOU ARE THE BRANCHES. IF YOU REMAIN IN ME AND I IN YOU, YOU WILL BEAR MUCH FRUIT; APART FROM ME YOU CAN DO NOTHING." JOHN 15:5 NIV

I t was a Monday morning like any other. I had even managed to leave for work a few minutes early, and the drive through the mountains was uneventful. I got off of the interstate to take my usual exit and pulled up to the first traffic light, stopping smoothly at the front of the line. The light turned green, and I instinctively moved my right foot from the break to the gas pedal. I heard the engine rev, but my nine-year-old SUV didn't move—not even a little bit.

My first thought was that I had done something wrong. Had I put the vehicle in park at the stop light without meaning to? I looked at the gear shift to make sure that it was still in drive. It was. I pushed the gas pedal harder this time and began to worry that the cars behind me would assume that I wasn't paying attention (because sometimes, I don't). I dreaded the honks that I was certain would soon be coming. Again, I heard the engine rev, but the SUV remained completely still. I looked for my hazard light button but couldn't find it. (I had never needed it before.) I looked to see if there were any warning lights on the dashboard, but there were none.

I turned the engine off completely and then turned it on again, hoping that perhaps the vehicle's computer chip simply needed to be rebooted. I repeated my steps at least three more times: foot to the gas pedal; rev the engine. You know what they say about "doing the same thing over and over again and expecting different results" (with "they" being Albert Einstein—or not).[1] Yep, "insanity." My SUV remained comatose. Finally, I saw the hazard button and pushed it, which I suppose was my way of admitting defeat.

I was so close to my destination, yet so far away. The clinic I work at was only minutes down the road. And just one-hundred yards away was Tires Plus, the "total car care" location that I had taken my SUV to for the state inspection that had been required when I moved to Maryland three years earlier. I called my nurse Anna, and she sent another co-worker, Bill, to pick me up in her Jeep (because he'd driven his motorcycle to work). Next, I requested a tow truck before calling the police. A deputy came and called the tow truck company again himself to ensure that they would arrive promptly, since my vehicle was obviously blocking traffic. It was now twenty minutes past my first patient's scheduled appointment time, and the clock was still ticking.

As I stood there on the curb with Bill, waiting for a tow truck to move my SUV just a few hundred feet away, I hoped that the problem wouldn't be too costly. Bill hoped along with me. "Maybe, it's just a computer problem," he said—trying to be optimistic for my sake—after first revealing that the one time he'd had a similar experience, it proved to be a dead transmission. "I knew I shouldn't have taken that old Honda on a trip to Florida, because it already had 300,000 miles on it," he shared regretfully.

Since my SUV only had 129,000 miles on it, I continued to wish for an easier and less dramatic malfunction.

After leaving my key for the mechanic at Tires Plus and riding the rest of the way to work with Bill, I started my clinic day—now halfway through my second patient's appointment slot—and waited for news about the health of my vehicle. A few hours later, the call came. The administrative assistant relayed the news, and by the tone of her voice, I knew that it wasn't going to be good. She actually sounded as if she was about to tell me that someone had died. "It's the transmission," she summarized in her death notification before giving me her condolences, "I'm really sorry...."

Still naive to the gravity of the situation, I broke her silence. "Doesn't anyone ever fix the transmission?" She responded with another apology. "Uhm, I'm sorry. I didn't mean to imply that you can't replace the transmission, if you really want to keep this car. It's just that I see a lot of people hop from car to car when even *less* goes wrong, and I don't usually see them replace the transmission."

I would later understand the reason for her somber, pity-laden pronouncement of vehicular death. The process of replacing the transmission was too complicated for their business to even provide me with an estimate, although they were used to doing all sorts of repairs. Evidently, the story would have to be continued, as I called *another* tow truck to take the SUV just a few miles up the road to the Buick dealer. Soon enough, there were two tow truck bills and two diagnostic fees, but I was given only one diagnosis: the transmission was shot.

The price of a resolution was hard to justify. Sure, I could buy a new transmission for $6,300. But first, I would need to pick my jaw up off the floor (and wipe a tear from the corner of my eye), since I had just discovered that my beloved SUV was now worth *less* than the cost of the replacement transmission itself. My trust in Buick was also faltering. What if I splurged on a new transmission, only to experience another costly problem just a few months later?

Door number two in my game show-reminiscent experience was a *used* transmission with 120,000 miles already on it—and a price tag of $3,300. The warranty was good for 12,000 miles, which in my particular case would only last about seven months due to the length of my daily commute. My husband and I took a night to think about our two options, neither of which sounded very appealing. The next morning, we still didn't feel good about either decision. We were at an impasse, it seemed, and neither of us wanted to go any further.

In spite of the fact that starting over with a new vehicle would mean making monthly car payments once again, it still appeared to be the safer bet. At least our money would be going toward reliable transportation with an extended warranty. So, we cut our losses, and my automotive companion of nine years was sold to CarBrain *as-is* for just $700 less than it would have been worth to Carmax if it had still contained a working transmission. The following week, we bought a new car from Toyota, the company who had made our 2008 Sienna that cost *half* as much and is still going strong at 220,000 miles (albeit with signs of its age that've led to a nickname of Tan Van and some obligatory jokes at its expense during family rides).

I can still see the beautiful, silver Buick Enclave, sitting at the very last stop light she would ever pull up to. If you didn't know what had happened, you would never imagine that she was literally paralyzed—damaged beyond any reasonable repair and broken from within due to a terminal diagnosis. How could something that was dead inside appear so elegant and good-looking on the outside? I thought back to the day that my husband had found her for me. Out of love, he had decided that I needed something better and more expensive than the vehicle I had initially been interested in.

In the hopes of making a sale, the Buick dealer allowed Jason to take the Enclave to the parking lot of the hospital where I worked, and it didn't take long for both of us to fall in love with the nearly $50,000 luxury vehicle that seemed to have Martz written all over it. The Buick Enclave had it all: a gorgeous body, heated leather seats, seating for seven, *two* sunroofs, a DVD player, separate air conditioning and heating controls for the driver and passenger sides, memory seats to remember the position preference of two different drivers, a hitch that came standard, and many more features that I had never known about before (but suddenly seemed necessary).

They say that beauty fades, and that it is what's on the inside that really matters. But what if the beauty *hasn't* faded, and it is what's on the inside that is worn out instead? Until the day that my luxury vehicle died, I didn't even know what a transmission was. Now that it's gone, I realize how critical its job is. According to the Oxford Dictionary, the transmission provides "the mechanism by which power is transmitted from an engine to the wheels of a motor vehicle." No wonder my wheels wouldn't move at that green light, though the engine was releasing the power that they needed. Without a working transmission, the wheels simply couldn't receive the engine's power. I had revved that engine over and over and could hear that even *more* power was being sent than usual, but this power, too, was expended in vain.

So many spiritual parallels came to mind. How worthless my stunning Buick Enclave was now, with all of her costly, unnecessary bells and whistles. What good are beauty and luxury if they can't transmit the engine's power to the road and perform the critical task of providing the transportation that we buy a vehicle for in the first place? I thought about myself. Am I really much better than my Enclave sometimes?

I do all sorts of things to ensure that I look good on the outside. Beauty isn't going to happen without a little help, after all—and that help requires time, money, and even the power to resist. The checklist is endless, so I'll give you the short version: trips to the hair salon, new clothes and shoes to keep up with the latest trends, whitening toothpaste, and self-control when I desperately want seconds on dessert. And then there is my reputation. I want *that* to be flawless, too, of course. I do my best to get positive patient reviews and outstanding clinical evaluations. But more than anything, I crave the respect of my colleagues, so that I can feel worthy in *their* eyes especially.

But what about my insides—the only thing that really matters in the eyes of Heaven? It seems that my heart is my best part. I *want* to do right and make God proud. The apostle Paul wanted to do the same. If only my good intentions were transmitted to my hands, feet, and lips with a perfect record. Even the Enclave was able to accomplish that for nine years, so why can't I? It would be easy to get discouraged, if I thought I was unique in my failure. Thank goodness for Paul's honest confession: "I don't really understand myself, for I want to do what is right, but I don't do it. Instead, I do what I hate" (Rom. 7:15 NLT).

I need a reliable *spiritual* transmission—someone who can help me turn my good desires into deeds of righteousness. Where can I find this transmission that I so desperately need? Truly, I am junkyard ready without it. My "...righteous acts are like filthy rags" (excerpt from Isaiah 64:16 NIV). And if I find it, surely it would be costly. How would I ever be able to afford it?

Enter a Savior. He came before I would even know that I needed Him. Jesus Christ is the greatest, most reliable transmission that has ever existed. Only He can take our best-laid plans to follow His commandments and transmit them into genuine, consistent action. His transmission is trustworthy, of course, but none of that would matter if the price tag was out of our reach. It should be (out of our reach, that is). For the cost—the life of the Transmission Himself—is priceless. But He paid it in full anyways. And He only asks for two things in return: our love and devotion. Even these two things, He gave us first.

Chapter Twenty-Seven

SMOKE INCOGNITO

"FOR THE HEARTS OF THESE PEOPLE ARE HARDENED, AND THEIR EARS CANNOT HEAR, AND THEY HAVE CLOSED THEIR EYES—SO THAT THEIR EYES CANNOT SEE, AND THEIR EARS CANNOT HEAR, AND THEIR HEARTS CANNOT UNDERSTAND, AND THEY CANNOT TURN TO ME AND LET ME HEAL THEM. BUT BLESSED ARE YOUR EYES, BECAUSE THEY SEE; AND YOUR EARS, BECAUSE THEY HEAR." MATTHEW 13:15-16 NLT

It was the crackling campfire sounds that first alerted me to the fact that something was wrong. We often used the fire pits in our yard, but instinctively, I knew that this familiar sound did not belong *inside* my house. I jumped up from the family room couch where I had been talking with my mother. And then I saw the horrifying sight on the kitchen stove. The large plastic Tupperware container that held the four dozen, made-from-scratch chocolate chip cookies that my daughter Makenzie had worked so hard to make the night before now lie half-melted on the burner.

Thick smoke was rising from the stovetop—not to be outdone by the sparks of fire that were making popping noises.

I heard a scream. (Was that me?) A cry for help came next, and although I repeated my plea twice, only my mother came, because no one else could hear me. I knew that there was a fire extinguisher in the house, but I couldn't remember where we keep it. (Note to self: there is no point in owning a fire extinguisher if it's going to be MIA when a fire actually occurs.) I knew that we needed a back-up plan, and clearly, I was desperate. Water seemed like the next best thing, so I turned on the kitchen sink and grabbed the pull-out sprayer. I tugged on it until it could grow no longer, and then I aimed it at the fiasco in front of me. It calmed things down but made an even bigger mess—and the Tupperware continued to burn.

Just then, my girls showed up with the fire extinguisher, whose location had been revealed to them by my husband during their recent frantic phone call. Murphy's Law. He wasn't home and learned about the disaster that was happening in his home just as he was about to be called from the waiting room at his doctor's office. Of course, the show must go on. I grabbed the fire extinguisher, pointed it at the stove and pulled the trigger, sweeping the nozzle back and forth over the smoldering cookies that we had just said rivaled those of the famous Mrs. Field hours earlier.

Finally, the burning stopped. But I knew that we were still in danger. Before we could clean up the daunting mess before us, we would need to tackle and eliminate one more enemy: the lingering smoke. The kitchen air was now the color of charcoal, yet it wasn't the pigment that bothered me most. I could literally *feel* the smoke in my lungs. My eyes burned, too. I tried to open the window above the kitchen sink, but it wouldn't budge. I ran to the windows behind the kitchen table, and thankfully, they opened easily! My sons went on a rescue mission to find the pets and then brought them into an upstairs bedroom. With our dog and three cats now safe and secure, we flung open every door of the house, hoping that the smoke would exit—even if it meant that the flies I detest could now freely enter.

The four of us went outside and sat on the front steps to escape the smoke, if only for a moment. We could breathe! How good it felt to experience something so basic that we normally take for granted. "We survived," my mother declared in relief, as she tried to get us to look at the bright side. Still pessimistic myself, I let my inner thoughts slip out. "Hopefully, we don't die in an hour or two from the smoke inhalation we've already experienced." After a two-minute dose of clean air, we headed back into the kitchen. I began to cough immediately, and my chest burned once again.

Over the next hour, we alternated unpleasant minutes of cleaning the overwhelming stove mess in our smoke-filled kitchen with satisfying minutes of inhaling fresh air during coveted escapes to the front steps outside. Once the stove was finally clean, we tackled the adjacent countertops, which had become covered with a thick layer of gray powder that I assume had formed from a mixture of the toxic, unwanted smoke and the chemicals from the fire extinguisher that had neutralized it. When that was finally gone, there was *still* more to do. We realized that the dry powder from the extinguisher had also made its way onto the island, the wooden floor, and even the table at the farthest end of the kitchen. *Everything* had to be cleaned—some of it twice. It felt like we would never be finished. But eventually, we were. The kitchen appeared clean once again. Appeared, I say, because it sure didn't smell that way.

The smell of the smoke was still quite strong. And our best attempts to remove it didn't seem to make any difference. We brought the high-powered air purifier from our bedroom down to the kitchen and turned it on full blast—the air purifier with the charcoal filter inside it that we had specifically chosen fifteen years earlier because we lived in a small apartment with a chain smoker next door. It had successfully removed the cigarette smoke that routinely drifted into our bedroom from the shared pipes in our master bathroom and threatened the lungs of our newborn baby, Makenzie. But even with a new filter, it was no match for the invisible Smoke Beast that now lingered in our kitchen. Although we could no longer see him, he seemed to have attached himself with tentacles to every nook and cranny of the room. If I wanted to be in my kitchen, I simply had to share it with him.

As the days passed, I noticed something that I hadn't expected. Each time I walked into the kitchen from another room, the smell of smoke would immediately grab my attention—just as it had before. But after I had stayed a while, I couldn't perceive it anymore. Over and over, the same thing happened: Leave. Come back. Smell smoke. Stay a while. Believe I'm actually smelling clean air. The spiritual parallel nearly hit me in the face.

Is this what I've been doing with the rest of my life—recognizing sin when I first come into contact with it and then staying so long that it no longer appears to be sin at all? I knew that it was true, as examples from my past flashed back to my memory. How many times have I needed to believe that something I wanted to do was acceptable before God—and then told myself that it was? Too often, I have become comfortable with sin by simply allowing myself to be near it. How easy it then becomes to rationalize away the things in the Bible that contradict my cherished desires and beliefs.

Just as my nose could no longer smell the smoke that was leaving its scent on me once I had been near it for even a little while, my senses, too, become dulled by sin the longer I'm around it. How then can I recognize sin for what it is? Staying away from it in the first place is the obvious move. If only I could do that consistently enough to keep from sinning. But alas, I am drawn to sin like a bee is drawn to honey. So, I will always need a Savior to rescue me from it.

If I am to be redeemed, however, there is one thing I must do. I alone can decide to listen to the Holy Spirit when He speaks. So often, the Bible talks about eyes that cannot see and ears that cannot hear. And in each case, the implication is made that the blindness and deafness to spiritual truths developed at the will of people themselves. For some of them, there was likely a spirit of stubbornness and resistance from the very beginning. But for others, their eyes and ears closed very slowly—only after they simply failed to respond to the Holy Spirit's wooing time after time.

Perhaps some of them had even planned to listen to God's voice *later*, but later didn't come before they lost their ability to listen altogether. This is what I fear and want to guard against in my own life. So, I depend on Christ to help me even with the responsibility that is technically my own. "Don't give up on me," I say to Him silently within my heart. "Don't ever stop trying to reach me," I add for good measure. And I am certain that He won't.

Chapter Twenty-Eight

IT'LL BE OKAY IN THE END

"THE LORD IS CLOSE TO THE BROKENHEARTED;
HE RESCUES THOSE WHOSE SPIRITS ARE CRUSHED."
PSALMS 34:18 NLT

As soon as I arrived home from work, I found my oldest daughter, Meliah, sitting at the kitchen table smiling, obviously ready to tell me about her good news. "I made Varsity," my high school senior shared with excitement, as her father stood nearby. She had been attending volleyball practices all summer, along with her younger sister. Suddenly, she stopped gushing, and I watched a look of seriousness replace the expression of happiness that had just been on her face. "Kenni didn't make Varsity," she announced rather quietly (using one of the nicknames she gave her sister). "She's really disappointed. I want to be happy that I made it—but I feel bad for her, and I don't want to make her feel worse." I nodded in understanding and then told her, "You can celebrate with me and Dad when Makenzie isn't around. It's very thoughtful of you to think of her feelings." I knew that Meliah actually understood her sister's emotions from firsthand experience.

Memories of the start of Meliah's 6th grade year came flooding back. She had tried out for the Varsity volleyball team at her school in Tennessee years earlier and had been so excited the day she knew that the results of the tryouts would be posted. Though I normally dropped the kids off at school without getting out of the car, I had parked my car on that particular morning so that I could look at the team lists with her. Meliah ran ahead of me to the hallway and glanced at the paper on the wall, so full of hope. I walked faster, so that I could look with her, but before I could catch up and scan the list myself, I saw my child's face fall.

In an instant, the hope was replaced with disappointment. I watched as Meliah tried to hide her sadness from the girls who were swarming around her. As tears welled up in her eyes, she carefully avoided making eye contact with any of her classmates and retreated to the bathroom. I followed and stood by as she splashed water on her eyes and then tried to dry them with the stiff brown paper towels, so that no one would know she'd been crying. "I'm okay, Mom," she attempted to reassure me. But I knew that she wasn't—and frankly, neither was I.

I didn't need my daughter to be on the team for my own gratification, as some parents do. You would never see me on an episode of Toddlers & Tiaras.[1] And I'm certainly no Wanda Holloway either.[2] Yet, I was crushed all the same. For I cannot bear to watch my kid experience heartache.

As I said good-bye to Meliah and drove the rest of the way to work that morning, this mama's heart felt heavier—and yet more fragile—than usual. Neither of us could possibly know that she would be moved up to the Swing team within two weeks, which allowed her to play in some of the Varsity games though she was also on the Junior Varsity team. (That sure was good news.) But I did understand one thing even from the very beginning, as I watched my daughter's heart sink the day the original teams were posted: her pain would not last forever. As a 6th grader with limited life experiences, she didn't have the ability to see that yet. Only someone who had lived decades more—and seen firsthand how quickly the years pass and situations change—could know that.

And now the 18-year-old Meliah standing in front of me knew it, too. "Kenni will be okay," she declared with confidence. "She'll make Swing or Varsity before she knows it. There's still time before she graduates. I told her that, but she's still really sad. She wouldn't even eat supper tonight." I reminded my maturing daughter about her experience as a 6th grade grader, and then I added, "It's hard to understand that things will get better one day when you're in the middle of the disappointment—especially when you're young. Everything in the future seems so far away." Meliah nodded in understanding. "I'm so happy for you that you made the Varsity team this year," I said, as I hugged her tightly. And then I headed upstairs to see the 15-year-old daughter of mine who *hadn't*—in spite of the fact that she had attended more summer practices than her sister.

I found Makenzie in her room, lying in bed in the dark without any covers on. Since she was facing the wall, I couldn't tell if she was actually asleep. But I suspected that she wasn't, because the sleep machine from my own adolescence that she loves so much had not been turned on. I climbed into her bed and got as close to her as I could—so that my stomach was touching her back—and then I put my right leg on hers so she could feel that I was with her. Very intentionally, I said nothing, as I rubbed her arm and stroked her hair. Minutes passed, and I continued my attempts to comfort her in silence, knowing that this is what she needed most—and t he *only* smart thing that Job's friends in the Bible had actually done.

Finally, I spoke into the dark room as I continued to stroke my sweet girl's hair. "I heard about Varsity, Honey. I'm so sorry...." Eventually, I heard my child cry ever so quietly, but unmistakably. I wrapped my arm around her more tightly and tried to think of something better to say. "I know it feels like forever until you'll get your turn—and that it's terrible to be on this side of things."

Meliah pushed the door open a bit and whispered, "Are you going to come hang out with me in your room soon?" Even at 18 years of age, it was still her Friday night tradition to cuddle with her mama. "I can't leave yet," I whispered to her. Little Ryder stopped by next, and I told him the same thing. I knew that my Makenzie needed me most—although she hadn't even asked me to come. So that was where I was going to be.

Soon I heard Carson, Meliah, and Ryder laughing and screaming as they ran back and forth in the hallway and nearby upstairs rooms playing their usual random Friday night games. I was glad that they were getting along—but in my attempts to protect Makenzie, I asked them to be quiet. It's not easy to hear the sounds of joy in others' lives when our own hearts are experiencing letdown.

I stayed with Makenzie a little longer, alternating periods of silence with the best words of encouragement that I knew how to give. Although she never said a word, I knew that she was listening. And while I cannot remember everything that I said to her that disheartening night, I will never forget the words I left her with: "I promise that it'll be okay in the end—even if it's not okay now." It had taken me forty-four years and many painful experiences to learn this reality myself—a reality that could only be true because Jesus had sacrificed everything to make it possible.

I thought back to the times when things looked bleak in my own life because I couldn't see past the situation I was in at that moment and believed that time would pass ever so slowly. Heartbreak over unwanted break-ups and broken promises. Lonely singleness that seemed like it would last forever. Two years of infertility and recurrent miscarriage that brought unexpected grief and made it feel like motherhood would never come. Two years of watching my child go through hell on earth as she required a bone marrow transplant that we were told could possibly kill her—though without it, she would surely die. Six months without a diagnosis for another child with a life-altering neurological disease that some doctors made her feel was in her head before the rare autoimmune disease was finally identified. Years more of a treatment for this rare disease whose side effects rivaled the modest benefit it provided. An unexpected diagnosis for my youngest child when he was only in kindergarten—one that has no cure and will lead to progressive neurological damage in his spinal cord and legs that he will have to live with for the rest of his life.

Through all of it, I heard God whispering to me, "I promise that it'll be okay in the end—even if it's not okay now." Sometimes, the "okay" came just a few years later, and the time of heartache was short enough. But other times, I know that the "okay" He has promised me will only come in t he *next* life—the eternal one in Heaven—when this life of sin and sorrow can't hurt me or my children anymore. Like a mother who cannot bear to watch her child experience the heartbreak of not making the Varsity volleyball team, the God of the Universe cannot bear to watch us suffer. And although He knows that our suffering is temporary—just as I knew that my daughter's would be—He still understands that for His children, the sadness runs deep in those moments.

How difficult it must have been for God to watch me cry in those trials that only He knew were temporary. How much He must've wanted to show me the better future that lie ahead, although He knew that He couldn't. And *this* is why He has asked me to trust Him. For He knows that it is only by trusting Him that I am able to feel the comfort He so desperately wants to give me. It is the same comfort that He gave to His Son in His own time of anguish in the Garden of Gethsemane—and it's the same comfort that He wants to give *you* the very next time you need it.

CHAPTER TWENTY-NINE

THE LIGHT BEHIND THE CLOUDS

"THIS IS MY COMMAND—BE STRONG AND COURAGEOUS! DO NOT BE AFRAID OR DISCOURAGED. FOR THE LORD YOUR GOD IS WITH YOU WHEREVER YOU GO." JOSHUA 1:9 NLT

The moon was larger-than-life that night. As I was driving home from work on my usual route—my mind and body on autopilot—it caught my attention immediately because its appearance was so unique. Its size? *Ginormous.* Its shape? Perfectly round. Its color? Golden-orange. Its brightness? More radiant than I had ever seen in my forty-four years. The best word that I can think of to summarize its grand splendor? **Breathtaking**. I wanted to capture its beauty forever with my iPhone's camera, but alas, taking pictures while driving is generally frowned upon (and admittedly, for good reason). So, I tried to soak in the images of the real thing for as long as possible, hoping that the memory of its beauty would be imprinted on my brain permanently.

All too soon, the special showing of Nature's art gallery was over. And I wasn't even home yet. I watched with disappointment as multiple fluffy clouds covered this exceptionally brilliant moon—and suddenly, my luminous friend was gone. At first, I thought that I would see him again soon. Surely, the clouds would roll on by, or he would outpace them instead. I waited patiently for the moon to show himself again. But alas, I waited in vain. With my light no longer visible, I drove the rest of the way home in the dark—and as I did, the black sky brought me back to a time when it seemed like God had exited the stage of my life and taken the light with Him.

It was 2016, and I was faced with an unexpected trial. First, I had tried to help myself. And then when that didn't work, I had reached out to others for help. When the first individual couldn't do anything to make the situation better, I sought help from another . . . and another—all the while praying for Divine intervention. But nothing changed. If anything, my suffering got worse.

Nothing had gone the way I'd wanted it to—the way that I was certain *He* had wanted it to go, too. "Where are you anyways, God?" I had asked with all sincerity. "I trusted You—and look where it got me?" The darkness was all that I could see. Like the massive moon that I had watched disappear behind the clouds that now masked its magnificent glow, my God's light appeared to have gone out before my problem had even been solved. As the very last visible door closed figuratively in my face—and it became clear that all human avenues of hope were now exhausted—I felt *moonless*.

And then, I remembered.... I remembered the other seemingly-unanswered prayers and moonless times when I thought the light would never return. Amidst those unwanted moments, there were so many different emotions. Sadness and loneliness. Worry and disappointment. But none of these emotions was the worst one I experienced. That prize goes to anger. For it was anger that once caused me to walk away from God for an entire year in 2001. Of course, I was in the wrong. (And that is a story for another chapter.)

My God proved to be faithful—even when I wasn't. Over and over, He has proved His faithfulness to me. Sometimes, He answered my prayers quickly—and He did it in the exact manner that I expected. But far more often, He made me wait much longer. And undoubtedly, the method He used was considerably better.

As I remembered these things one night in 2017–with my problem still very much unsolved and tears of frustration at both God and my situation welling up in my eyes—I finally surrendered. Sitting alone in my car, I made a declaration to God that evolved even as I thought it and spoke it. *Well, it looks like You've abandoned me on this one, God*, I proclaimed, knowing that Heaven could hear me even inside my head. *But I know that You're still here*, I acknowledged seconds later in a rebuttal of my own accusation. And then my heart finished the rest of its thought out loud. "I **know**," I said defiantly to my Defeat, as much as I said it to my God. They were just two words, but they were spoken boldly—both to myself and to the God that I had once abandoned.

Years have passed, and God has shown me why He didn't answer that prayer the way I wanted Him to in the beginning—and even assumed that He would. God is doing things a different way, and I have confessed to Him that the glimpse into His plan that He's given me has shown me that His way is far better than the one I had in mind. But this story isn't finished yet, and the more I get to know God, the more convinced I become that it won't be finished for years to come. After all, the Bible tells me that it's kind of His M.O. (aka His Modus Operandi). So that particular book of mine will have to wait.... And in the process, God is working on my weakest fruit of the spirit. Patient I was not, but patient I am actually becoming.

Sometimes, the light of the moon is hidden by the clouds. And when this happens, life is darker and feels harder to navigate than usual. But that doesn't mean that that the moon is gone. He didn't leave, and he isn't going to—just as God is still there when the clouds roll into our lives, and we can't see Him. I know that now, although it took me a while to realize it. Like the moon that shows up every night—no matter what's happening in this world—the God of the Universe (*and Multiverse*) is going to keep showing up for us. When we acknowledge His presence, He is there. And when we fail to recognize His presence, He is *still* there. I, for one, am so relieved that God's faithfulness doesn't depend on mine.

CHAPTER THIRTY

THE BILL WE CAN'T PAY

"FOR YOU KNOW THAT GOD PAID A RANSOM TO SAVE YOU FROM THE EMPTY LIFE YOU INHERITED FROM YOUR ANCESTORS. AND IT WAS NOT PAID WITH MERE GOLD OR SILVER, WHICH LOSE THEIR VALUE. IT WAS THE PRECIOUS BLOOD OF CHRIST, THE SINLESS, SPOTLESS LAMB OF GOD." 1 PETER 1:18-19 NLT

I t had been a *long* week, and I was ready for the weekend to begin that Friday afternoon even more than usual. Only one quick trip to the grocery store for a few essentials stood between me and the freedom of the Sabbath rest I craved. Because it was getting close to sundown, I stopped at a store I rarely shop at since it was close to work, and the grocery stores in my home town were still forty-five minutes away. I sped through the unfamiliar aisles with my cart and threw the wanted items in haphazardly as I raced to check out. Still in fast-paced mode and anxious to get home, I scanned the checkout lines to see which one was the shortest. As soon as I found the apparent winner, I took my place in line behind my fellow shoppers and settled in for what I assumed would be a fairly short wait.

I watched as the longer checkout lines on either side of me got shorter, while mine stayed the same. *Guess I picked the wrong one*, I thought to myself disappointedly as I looked at my watch. Another few minutes passed, but the line I was standing in still didn't move—not even a little bit. I craned my head around the line of carts and customers to see if I could identify the problem. It didn't take long.

A woman at the head of my line pulled out another card from her wallet and handed it to the clerk. "Try this one," she said, with a nervous look on her face that told me that the previous card had been declined. A minute later, the clerk handed her back card number two and said, "I'm sorry, but this one didn't work either." Obviously embarrassed, the woman apologized and looked like she wanted to disappear. "I don't know why it's not working," she responded. "There's still money on it. It should work...." Her voice trailed off.

The checkout clerk looked sympathetic but stuck. She appeared frazzled as she glanced at the line that was continuing to grow behind the one customer whose transaction she couldn't seem to complete. "Maybe someone in Customer Service can get the card to work," the grocery store employee suggested next, pointing to the counter that was twenty feet away. The woman nodded and started to push her cart full of groceries forward, but then she stopped and looked back at the rest of us to apologize. "I'm sorry that I held up the line."

With the source of the delay now removed, the line began to move quickly once again. I was glad to be one step closer to home and the start of my weekend, of course. But I didn't feel as relieved as I had thought I would. My eyes drifted over to the Customer Service desk. I could see the woman standing by as an employee in Customer Service held her debit card in one hand and the telephone in the other. I noticed that a man was standing close by with his hand on the woman's grocery cart. All three adults appeared weary.

The checkout clerk pulled my attention back to the line that I'd been waiting in for much longer than I had anticipated. It was finally my turn. I put my items on the conveyor belt, and she scanned them just as quickly. When the tally was complete, I put my own debit card inside the chip reader, and the machine read "approved" within a few seconds. I could go home at last.

I should've felt free, but something inside my heart kept me from heading straight for the parking lot. I knew what I needed to do—what God would *want* me up do. Perhaps, I had even come to the store I rarely shop at on this very night for such a time as this. I stopped at the Customer Service counter and spoke to the store employee first. "I'd like to pay for her groceries," I said quietly. She looked surprised but relieved, and then she hung up the phone. I handed the Customer Service employee my debit card and then looked at the woman whose cart full of unpaid-for-groceries was waiting close by. She thanked me, as I knew that she would—and then I stopped her. "I did this because God impressed me to do it, so please give Him the credit," I said, as I hoped that she would.

What happened next surprised me. With a big smile on her face, she called out to the man who'd been standing by her grocery cart and said with obvious excitement, "I told you that God would take care of us!" I was happily *stunned*. The grocery store employee caught my attention and handed me the chip reader, so that I could enter my PIN number. Four digits later, and the screen said, "Approved." And just like that, the bill that the woman and her boyfriend had been unable to pay was now paid in full.

As I pushed my own cart of groceries out to the parking lot, it felt like I was walking on cloud nine. Tears welled up in my eyes, and I wondered why it seemed like I was the one who had been given a gift. I thought about it on the drive home, and soon I understood the reason for my own joy. How lucky I was to have been used by God in this place on this night. That was part of it, yes. The gift of giving is truly *amazing*, just as they've always said it is. And the giving especially feels good when it's being done in the name of God. But there was more to it than that.

I was reminded that **I am the one with the bill I can't pay.** It is me who cannot afford the cart full of items that are needed to nourish and sustain my life. I am doomed to die with an unpayable debt hung around my neck. At best, I am a slave to sin. At worst, I am the sickness of sin itself. Either way, I cannot pay. I am in desperate need of a Redeemer. To say that I was lucky enough to have one come to my rescue would not be the truth. For luck had nothing to do with it.

Only love could lead a sinless One to redeem the life of a sinner before they were even asked. Love came to our rescue—yours and mine. Jesus Christ volunteered to pay our bill and redeem us when no one else could . . . or would. And this same love is why His Father allowed it. Walk on cloud nine with me now, my fellow debtors, for we have been redeemed. Love and obey this humble King with me, my fellow sinners, for we have been forgiven and blessed by the sacrifice that only Heaven could pay.

CHAPTER THIRTY-ONE

WHAT KIND OF FATHER WOULD SACRIFICE HIS SON?

"BUT GOD DEMONSTRATES HIS OWN LOVE FOR US IN THIS: WHILE WE WERE STILL SINNERS, CHRIST DIED FOR US." ROMANS 5:8 NKJV

I'd known Mr. Wonder* for a few years now, and we had always gotten along well. He'd been dealt two different autoimmune diseases—one that affected his kidneys and another that affected his eyes. Although the kidney disease was said to be in remission on medication, the damage had already been done. He was dependent on dialysis. As far as the unrelated vasculitis in his eyes goes, his vision had been declining. The first-line treatment couldn't be used, since it interacted with the drug that he still needed for the kidney disease—a disease that could also cause life-threatening hemorrhaging in his lungs, if left untreated.

One day, we discussed the reasons for his decision not to receive a COVID-19 vaccine. I listened as he shared his distrust of those involved: the drug companies who would obviously profit from its use financially, the government who was mandating its administration for employees in certain fields, and especially the politicians and news media outlets who were admittedly benefiting from the controversy in the form of increased votes and ratings on *both* sides. Although I wanted to cut through all of those things and convince him to take the vaccine that I knew could potentially save his life from what I had actually seen and also heard from my fellow physicians in the hospital trenches, I sensed that this particular patient wasn't going to change his mind no matter what I said. I kept silent as he continued to speak, and the conversation veered from its origins into a new tangent of distrust. Somehow, he had also learned to distrust the Bible.

I didn't know how our conversation had gotten here, but I knew that I had been presented with an opportunity to lead him to a Lifesaver that was even more effective than the COVID-19 vaccine that I still wanted him to have. One could potentially save his earthly life, while the other could save his *eternal* life. He continued to talk—and although I was short on time—I didn't stop him. "I used to go to church when I was a kid, but there are some things about God and the Bible that just don't make sense," he shared honestly. And now he had my full attention.

An expression of frustration formed on his face, and soon I knew why. "I have a family member who is a Christian, and I asked her two questions, but she couldn't really answer them and just got mad at me," Mr. Wonder remembered out loud. "What were they?" I asked on cue, hoping that I would be able to provide an answer he liked better (and with a different *spirit*, too). He didn't miss a beat. "I asked her why God supported incest."

It couldn't have been an easy one, could it? I lamented in the private conversation that I was having simultaneously inside my head.

A request for clarification seemed to be my best option for stalling the discussion, because I wasn't even certain what had prompted his question in the first place—although it clearly seemed genuine. "Can you explain what you mean?" I asked next. And then he told me what I needed to understand his specific concern. "Well, if the Bible is true, then Adam and Eve's children had incestuous relationships." *Aha*. I finally understood his thought process.

I didn't exactly argue with him, and I think that took him by surprise. "You're right. The Bible does say that Eve was the mother of all the living, so that must mean that her children had babies together." I did, however, attempt to provide some context. "But God didn't give any rules about what defined incest until at least two-thousand years later. Even Abraham was allowed to marry his half-sister, Sarah, though God later forbid marriage between half-siblings specifically. I've always been taught that one of God's reasons for doing this later was the fact that genetic mutations had accumulated over those first two millennia, and yet the people didn't understand that. God was wise to tell them not to marry their close relatives because they would have been more likely to have children with genetic conditions that require the same recessive mutation from *both* parents in order to cause the disease. Even cousins would have been more likely to share these same mutations—such as the ones that cause cystic fibrosis or sickle cell disease—but half-siblings would have been especially likely to carry the same mutation."

When he knew that I was finished, he proceeded to ask me the second question on his mind, which proved to be far more important. "If the Bible is true, then God allowed his own son to die. *Nobody* I know would do such a thing. What kind of father would a sacrifice his own son?"

And there it was. Bam! He had just asked the most critical question of an eternal lifetime. I prayed that my answer would do God justice, and then I attempted to answer the question that Mr. Wonder had been asking for years.

I started by complimenting the question itself. "You are very smart to have thought about this so deeply," I began. And then, I turned his question into the statement that has always made me love God as much as I do. "You are right," I acknowledged to Mr. Wonder that day. "No earthly father would sacrifice his son—especially for a bunch of ungrateful sinners. That's *exactly* what makes what God did so incredible and hard to comprehend. And in this case, the Son actually gave His consent. Only true love could have allowed either of them to do that for us."

We talked about other things that day—both medical and spiritual—but none will ever be as consequential as the question he asked me about what kind of father would sacrifice his son. It was incomprehensible to Mr. Wonder because it is truly incomprehensible to all of us. I suspect that even the angels in Heaven still cannot fully grasp the reason that their beloved Master was willing to make such a trade for unworthy sinners—or that His equally-loved Son consented to it all. And I am certain that Lucifer—now called Satan—never saw it coming.

I don't know if Mr. Wonder will change his mind about God because of our conversation, but I did ask him if it would be okay for me to send him a book that might help to answer his question in more detail. Because I am his physician, and I didn't want him to feel obligated to say yes, I promised Mr. Wonder that I would never ask him later if he had actually read it. He gave me his permission. Now the seed has been planted, and it is up to the Holy Spirit to water it. He can do amazing things with seeds.

*Name changed to protect the privacy of my patient

CHAPTER THIRTY-TWO

JESUS WEPT

"WHEN MARY REACHED THE PLACE WHERE JESUS WAS AND SAW HIM, SHE FELL AT HIS FEET AND SAID, 'LORD, IF YOU HAD BEEN HERE, MY BROTHER WOULD NOT HAVE DIED.' WHEN JESUS SAW HER WEEPING, AND THE JEWS WHO HAD COME ALONG WITH HER ALSO WEEPING, HE WAS DEEPLY MOVED IN SPIRIT AND TROUBLED. 'WHERE HAVE YOU LAID HIM?' HE ASKED. 'COME AND SEE, LORD,' THEY REPLIED. JESUS WEPT." JOHN 11:32-35 NIV

It was a new patient visit like no other. My nurse Angel had asked me a week earlier if it would be okay to convert the upcoming face-to-face visit to a telemedicine or video visit. This patient-to-be of mine, Mr. Hope*, had just been enrolled in hospice and wouldn't feel up to traveling to the clinic. I had agreed to the proposed visit conversion, of course, and thought no more about it. When the day and time of the appointment arrived, I clicked on the link to start the visit and saw that a woman was waiting for me on my screen.

At first, I didn't think much about it, as I often have male patients who would prefer to let their wives do most of the talking during our visits.

Since I hadn't met her before either, I asked if she was his wife, and she said yes. I didn't ask her where her husband was and simply let her talk.

Everything had changed just nine months earlier when he had noticed blood in his urine. He had sought medical attention immediately, but even with a prompt evaluation, the news wasn't good. Bladder cancer had been lurking inside his body for longer than he could've ever imagined. Mr. Hope's tumor caused him to hemorrhage from his bladder, and he soon became weak from the anemia that developed. After receiving multiple blood transfusions, he was able to undergo surgery first and then radiation.

Yet, the cancer continued to spread, and Mr. Hope sought a second opinion. But as it would turn out, he wasn't well enough to start any sort of chemotherapy—not even *palliative* chemotherapy, which is less intense and only designed to prolong life in cases where a cure is no longer possible. Instead, he was admitted to the hospital with congestive heart failure and given diuretics intravenously to remove the extra fluid from his body, so that he could breathe more easily. He was discharged from the hospital, but not with hope—because there wasn't any left to give. Not even the most modern medicine that the United States of America has to offer could save him. So, Mr. Hope traveled to spend his last days with his family. It was hospice's turn to care for him now.

This is the part of their story where I met them—on a computer screen—just one week after Mr. Hope had been enrolled in hospice. After listening to the details of the unexpected and unwanted journey they had been on thus far, I asked Mrs. Hope if her husband would feel up to talking with me for a few minutes. Her answer took me by surprise. "He can't communicate anymore. That's new as of this morning." The hospice nurse had increased his morphine dose earlier the same day.

I didn't know what to say at first. Although I have cared for dying patients since my days in medical school—and done my best to comfort the loved ones they were leaving behind—never before had I experienced a situation like this in the outpatient clinic setting with a patient and spouse that I had just met. "I'm sorry," I replied, wishing that I had something much more profound to say. Mrs. Hope surprised me again by turning her screen in a different direction and announcing, "Here he is." My patient was laying on his side in a hospital bed that was located in the middle of the living room.

Mr. Hope was clearly unconscious, yet his eyes were open. I decided to call his name and say hello—more for his wife's sake, since I knew he couldn't hear me. I told him that I wished I had been able to meet him sooner. And then Mrs. Hope turned the screen back around. I knew that there was nothing more that I could do for her husband. The visit was for *her*.

I asked Mrs. Hope to tell me something about her husband that she wanted me to know, whether it was about his time in the service or his life in general. She paused just briefly and then shared that he had always fought for what he knew was right—even if there were going to be negative consequences. After telling her that this said a lot about his character, I asked her how she was doing. "Okay," she replied, but I suspected that she chose this answer simply because it was the easiest one to provide—and that she knew, too, that there was nothing I could do to change the grim reality that she was facing. "My mother is here to support me," she added. "I'm glad you're not alone," I responded, feeling relieved that there was actually something positive that I could comment on.

And then I dared to ask the question that always feels like the elephant in the room when death is imminent, as it clearly was for her husband. "Do you have hope that you will see your husband again?" Mrs. Hope was caught off guard. Of that, I was certain. Perhaps it was because she didn't expect this question from a physician. But I sensed that she wasn't certain of the answer herself either, so I probed a bit more. "I hope you don't mind if I ask you if you have any spiritual preference or background?" She broke eye contact at first—and then she told me that the Protestant Christian church that she and her husband had been married in decades earlier was "just down the street."

There was only one thing left in my arsenal as a healer to offer, and ultimately, its real power doesn't belong to me. But I still wanted to do my part to connect her to the last source of hope that any of us really has in this too-fragile, sorrow-filled life. Remembering that I was not alone, I offered her the only thing I could: "Would it be okay if I prayed with you, Mrs. Hope?" She nodded and quietly said, "Yes."

I had no idea what I would say in this prayer. Quickly, and silently, I said my own prayer first. *Please give me the right words*, I asked, knowing that the Holy Spirit would. And then I opened up my mouth and heart and left the rest up to Heaven.

"Dear Jesus," I began, because it only felt right to address this prayer to Him, in particular. "You are the Great Physician—far better than me. I know that you are grieving with this family too, because that's exactly what You did when your friend Lazarus first died. You weren't crying because he was gone, since You knew what You were just about to do. You wept because You saw your other friends—his sisters Martha and Mary—grieving...."

And with those words spoken, I couldn't continue, because I began to weep. As I thought about the empathy of Jesus and the *real* reason that He wept that day—which wasn't what I'd always thought it was—I loved Him even more. And with His Holy Spirit in the midst of this moment—spanning two different states, thirty minutes apart, on one video visit—I couldn't help but weep. As I prayed about the shortest verse in the Bible, "Jesus wept"—and what I now understood it to mean so fully—I wept, too (John 11:35 NKJV). I had prayed with many patients over the years—most of whom I had known for much longer—but never had I wept before.

Now I was weeping with a stranger. After a minute that felt much longer, I was able to finish my prayer. "I know that You are weeping with Mrs. Hope and her family," I said confidently to our empathetic Savior. "Please comfort them and give them hope of a future where they will be with him again—never to be separated—and he will be well and whole. You are our only hope, Jesus. Thank You for dying on the cross so that this hope could even be possible. We love You. Amen."

When the prayer was over, I asked Mrs. Hope if there was anything else that I could do for her or her husband. "No. I think hospice has everything covered," she replied. And with that, we said our good-byes and turned off our video links. My heart was filled with mixed emotions. My patient was dying, and there was nothing I could do as an earthly physician. Yet, I had been given the opportunity to point his wife in the direction of the great Comforter, the only source of hope that any of us really has in this world—whether we've realized it yet or not. And that felt *amazing*.

*Name and some details changed to protect the privacy of my patient

Chapter Thirty-Three

THE UNREQUITED HUG

"And he said: 'Truly I tell you, unless you change and become like little children, you will never enter the kingdom of heaven. Therefore, whoever takes the lowly position of this child is the greatest in the kingdom of heaven. And whoever welcomes one such child in my name welcomes me.'" Matthew 18:3 NIV

I wasn't exactly new to this mother-of-teenagers gig, so I don't know why it took me by surprise like it did. But I really never saw it coming. And admittedly, I was completely unprepared. This kind of thing only happens to someone else, after all—*not* to me, and certainly not so soon. By the time I realized what was happening, it was already too late to stop the train that was careening towards me at full speed. I had only two choices. Get out of the way or get crushed. Actually, it felt like the two options weren't mutually exclusive, and I could still be crushed even if it did get out of the way.

Just one year ago—or two, perhaps—my oldest son Carson had still looked like a young boy. He had sounded like one too. Best of all, he smiled a lot and giggled about silly things, as young boys often do. Subconsciously, I thought that he would stay this way forever. Consciously, I assumed that I would at least have plenty of time to say good-bye. Good-bye, silly child with the boy face and high-pitched voice. Good-bye, child of the nightly back-scratching, bedtime songs, and mother-son, birthday sleepovers. Too many precious rituals have seen their final episode without me even knowing that it would be the last one.

All of a sudden, there it was—right in front of my face. A transition had occurred without me even noticing it. My young boy now looked and sounded like a teenager, although his thirteenth birthday was still months away. How had this happened at the age of just twelve? How had the universe allowed it to happen at all, when I wasn't ready yet?! And the physical changes weren't the only part that I struggled to grasp and accept, as I tried to catch up to the new reality of who my son was becoming.

My twelve-year-old no longer wanted to surround himself with many of the things that had once defined him in my eyes. His favorite color, green. Legos. The horsehead and gorilla costumes. Marvel movies. His book of the tall towers of the world. The bearded dragon he had begged me for. His younger brother…. And it wasn't just that his favorite things had changed. It seemed that he no longer had any favorites at all.

A smile-free, sometimes-sullen countenance now replaced the happy-go-lucky facial expression that used to greet me on my son's face. "Are you depressed?" I asked him, more than once. "No," he would reply each time, with a mixture of confusion and annoyance on his face. "Don't take it personally. It's just hormones," my husband would try to reassure m e. "*Mutant* teenage hormones," my mother-in-law would remind my husband about with a wink as she too tried to encourage me.

I could even hear my own father's words about me from the 1990s in my memory vault. "You're so sullen these days, and you always hole up in your room," he would say as he looked at me with a sad, frustrated look on his own face. Only now as a parent myself could I finally understand that he was missing his little girl when he said these things. As I thought about it, I began to feel bad about the sad moments that the adolescent version of myself had put my parents through.

These realizations should've made me feel better. My husband and I turned out alright in the end, after all. But I didn't feel better. Not *really*. How could I, when it felt like I didn't have the closeness with my oldest son anymore that I still craved?

The new relationship with my twelve-year-old consisted of his requests for new clothes and gallons of ice cream. He is growing rapidly, loves sweets, and doesn't have a bank account. So, it made sense that he would come to me for these things. But I wanted more. I wanted to *feel* that he still loved me—that I was more than just a means to fulfill his needs and wish lists. I wanted to spend time with him and not have him bail on the family movie nights he once enjoyed or leave the table during family meals as quickly as he can scarf down his food.

As my twelve-going-on-twenty-year-old man-child seemed to be pulling away more and more each month, I realized that I needed to do more to bridge the gap (that I shuttered to think might become a chasm). I believe Frances Bacon said it best: "If the hill won't come to Muhammad, Muhammad will go to the hill."[1] I took my tween on secret dates to the local Dunkin Donuts some Sunday mornings, just so I could spend time with him alone like we used to. I texted him from the grocery store each week to ask if there was anything else he wanted (besides the ingredients for his bearded dragon's gourmet salads and his standing order for two gallons of mint chocolate chip ice cream). I hugged him once or twice a day and told him that I loved him. Sometimes, his arms squeezed back, and I was lucky enough to hear him say, "I love you too." Other times, it felt like a one-person show.

Still, I kept trying, as memories of this child as a newborn in the hospital kept flashing back. Two glorious days we had spent alone together cuddling and having special one-way conversations in the post-partum unit of the hospital during that cold Martin Luther King, Jr. weekend back in 2009. More than once, I had texted my husband while he was at home with our girls just to tell him how much he was going to love this special new baby. Oh, how I wanted to go back to those moments now—even if it was just for a few minutes! But, of course, I couldn't.

Instead, I continued to initiate hugs once or twice a day, so that my Carson would at least know that I loved him (and our relationship wouldn't grow too cold). One morning, I moved in for a hug as he was coming down the stairs, and my son twisted his body away from me. My arms and my face fell simultaneously. "Uhm, okay," I mumbled quietly as I turned around and walked down the stairs. Outwardly, I looked unharmed—but inwardly, it felt like I'd been punched in the gut.

I drove to work and tried to forget about the whole thing. For the first time in a while, I was grateful for the busyness of my workload because it took my mind off of the events of the morning. When I finally got home at 8 o'clock, something happened that I hadn't expected. My son approached me and apologized. "I'm sorry I wouldn't hug you this morning, Mom. I was just in a bad mood." "It's okay," I replied to the simple words that had immediately been a balm to my wounded heart. "I appreciate you saying that."

I'd like to say that this was the only time that my taller-than-his-mother-now, tween son rejected my attempts to hug him. But that would be a lie, for it happened again just a couple of months later. I'd also like to say that at least it hurt less the second time because my heart had grown tougher. But that too would be a lie. I drove to work feeling heavyhearted once again as I contemplated *never* initiating another hug. Why put myself out there and risk getting hurt again? I wondered if he would apologize when I got home, as he had the last time following the previous unrequited hug—but an apology never came.

The *kid* in me wanted to be passive-aggressive and stop doing the things for him that he had come to expect. *Let's just see how you like it when the ice cream doesn't show up and the orthodontics bill doesn't get paid*, I thought in my head. But none of these thoughts made me feel any better—or more in control. Instead, they made me feel as if I was playing the role of a jilted friend, rather than a mother. And I didn't like it. I didn't like it at all. I wanted to be like one of those perfect television moms, but I didn't know how.

One night, I went off script completely. An hour earlier, my son had told me (*again*) that I was annoying. And all I had done was put an air freshener in his room by his bearded dragon's cage. After claiming that the odor I had smelled bothered him *less* than the scent of the highly reviewed Renuzit Pure Breeze Pet product I had bought for him as an intended favor, the 12-year-old boy in my life spoke the words that were becoming all too familiar. "You're so annoying, Mom."

Of course, I knew that every kid thinks their mother is annoying at times. I had been a kid myself once, after all (sorry, Mom). But I had never been gutsy enough to speak these feelings out loud to my own mother. At least I'd like to remember it that way. (Perhaps *my* mother would tell you otherwise?)

Later that same night, when my son wandered into my bedroom, I couldn't help myself. The words I now regret came right out of my mouth without restraint. "Carson, you say that I'm annoying, but you can be annoying too, you know. You think you don't ever do anything that annoys me? And some of the things that you say are hurtful. I have real feelings, by the way." He said nothing—perhaps because he didn't know how to respond to the words that only made me feel better for a moment.

My thoughts drifted back to my Momaw. I had spent my childhood visiting her and Popaw—my mother's parents—in North Carolina. Each fifteen-hour drive from Massachusetts every May and December was filled with excitement, as I looked forward to all of the fun that I knew we'd have together. Sometimes, we would go on to visit places with built-in entertainment, such as camp meeting at Lake Junaluska or the mall in Charlotte, an hour away, that had its own ice-skating rink. But mostly, our good memories were made within the walls of my grandparents' small, television-less, one level home. My Momaw and Popaw *lived for* our visits and cried each time we left. I loved spending time with them, too—and for my Momaw, in particular, I would leave handwritten love notes on the inside of her kitchen cabinet doors for her to find after we were gone. She felt loved, and so did I.

But then the little girl who had once been so close to her grandmother grew up. The responsibilities along the road to becoming a doctor consumed her—although she didn't want them to. Her Popaw passed away in his early 70s somewhat unexpectedly, and it seemed like there was no time to even get away for his funeral. Each missed nineteen-hour day of pre-med classes and non-stop studying would be impossible to make up, it seemed, and no amount of additional sacrifice of her sleep could change that. Her mother didn't expect her to come either. And so, she poured out her heart—and tears—into a tribute that her mother promised to read at her grandfather's memorial service.

The next several years, the half-girl, half-woman only saw her Momaw a handful of times. And between those visits, there was no communication. No phone calls. No letters. Even when the visits did come, their relationship was different. The widowed grandmother would say each time, "I never see you anymore." And instead of feeling empathy for her loneliness, her granddaughter secretly felt annoyed. Their relationship was a far cry from the one they'd had with she was a child—and she could've never understood then what it was like for her grandmother to have felt forgotten.

I'd like to say that this story had a happy ending—that I matured and became less selfish before it was too late. But our story ended very differently. One day, the Momaw I had loved so deeply as a child was gone, without warning. No chance to say good-bye or tell her that I loved her still—and had loved her all along.

As I thought about my Momaw and my 12-year-old's changing needs and how they made me feel, I knew that he still loved me. I remembered the words that he had spoken just months earlier during our annual mother-son birthday sleepover (which he had told me would be our very last, since 13-year-old boys don't have sleepovers with their moms). Out of the blue, he had said, "You told Dad that you thought we didn't need you or love you anymore." Immediately, I felt embarrassed that my thoughts of self-pity from months earlier had become known, and the memories of that particular day came flooding back.

One Sunday, something I had said or done had irritated a couple of my older children, and they had told me so. Voices were raised, although I can't even remember the subject matter anymore. (So how important could it have been?) I had gone to bed early and cried myself to sleep. Only my youngest child still seemed to notice if I was home—instead of at work. Only he still followed me around when I was actually home and spontaneously said, "I love you, Mom." The others used to do these things, too—before they had more birthdays.

For some reason, the change in my relationships with the older kids had hit me hard that night, and my husband had asked me what was wrong. As my fears spilled out, he tried to reassure me. And then later on, he had shared my feelings with the girls, who had subsequently spread the news to their 12-year-old brother. He had kept the information to himself but filed it away in his heart.

Then later during that final mother-son, birthday sleepover, he informed me, "If you died, I would be sad for the rest of my life. You're my *mother*." My independent, tween boy of few words talked nonstop that night and revealed thoughts that told me he was more mature—and spiritually-minded—than I had realized. How I wished I could have stopped time and made that night last much longer. But the morning came right on time—and then all too soon, it was over.

Just as the morning after the ball must have felt like to Cinderella—when she was back in her old, shabby clothes and cleaning the fireplace once again—so it felt to me that next morning after we awoke from our final sleepover. My half-boy, half-man child went back inside his shell and returned to the world where it appeared that nothing—and no one—mattered to him. It was hard to return to the soot and loneliness, but I could not forget the magic of the "ball" and what my child had told me that I really mean to him. Undoubtedly, that brought me comfort. Yet, I wanted more. I wanted *every* day to be like the night of our sleepover had been. I wanted a living, breathing relationship with my son. Just as the food that I ate last month cannot sustain me indefinitely, that one night of bonding with my child—however wonderful—cannot fill the Carson-shaped hole in my heart forever.

That's exactly how I feel about you, I heard God whisper to my heart as I pondered these things. I thought about the many times in the Old Testament of the Bible when God Himself had craved the love and loyalty of the Israelites whom He'd first loved and wooed Himself. Although He already owns everything in the Universe and has limitless power—things we can only dream about—what matters to Him most is our love and affection.

Have you ever thought about how amazing that is? It's truly incomprehensible. Who am I that the God of *everything* should care about whether or not I love Him? How wonderful and truly undeserved it is that God's feelings should be affected by mine! What a responsibility, I realized, then lies with me as well. Just as I don't want the husband that I love to feel neglected or have to wonder if I still love him, neither do I want the God I love to ever have to miss my expressions of love for Him.

Though He may have the love and attention of a million other souls on this planet—and infinitely more angels in Heaven—God still wants *mine*. I thought about how happy it makes me when my firstborn, Meliah, still asks me at the age of eighteen, "Can we cuddle?" Or how wonderful it is when my Makenzie and Ryder ask to go on dates with me? The joy that I feel in these moments with these four children is so great that it cannot even be measured.

And yet, I am incomplete. If I am gifted with a thousand hugs and *I love yous* from these beloved kids, but there is distance between me and just *one* of my children, I will not be whole. Jesus revealed that He feels the same way when He told the story of the lost sheep. Although He was still surrounded by ninety-nine perfectly good sheep—and the one that was missing wasn't inherently more valuable than the others—His heart could not rest until He brought this lone sheep back home.

Jesus showed us that God Himself feels the same way by sharing the parable of the Prodigal son, whose father stood on his porch looking for his missing son. It didn't matter that he still had another son at home who hadn't become lost very intentionally, like the child he longed for had. No doubt he would've been standing on the porch, just the same, if the son at home had been the one who'd left instead. Each son's very existence caused their father to love them and desire a relationship with them. And he craved this bond even in the case of the one who had hurt him deeply.

Having been both a child and a parent myself now, I can finally understand what Jesus meant when He said in the book of Mark (in chapter 10, verses 14 and 15) that the Kingdom of God belongs to children—and that we must become like them, if we want to be a part of this kingdom. The best version of myself was the one who trusted God without any doubts or strings attached. The one who preached sermons to stuffed animals inside her bedroom when she was supposed to be napping (with the usual message being that "kids can preach just as good as grown-ups"). The one who never thought about politics. The one who poured out more love to her Momaw than she did to herself. The one who was a *child*....

"Come back, little Carson," I wanted to say each time I saw the older boy who no longer seemed to want to be part of my world. Instead, I paid a visit to his room (aka his private castle) and asked him, "Is there something that I could do better to make you want to hang out with me more like you used to? Or something I could do that would make you find me less annoying?" (*This* particular question was especially important, since annoying seemed to be his new favorite adjective for me.) I really had no idea how he would respond, or whether I should even be asking such a question to my 12-year-old.

Luckily, I saw his face soften, and he replied without hesitation, "There is nothing you could do better. You're doing everything fine. The problem is with me—not you." His unexpected words were a medicine to my soul, and I hoped that I would remember them the next time I was tempted to take it personally when he acted like the 12-year-old boy he actually is.

"Carson loves you still," my ever perceptive 8-year-old-son Ryder declared, soon after I asked him if *he* would still want to hang out with me when he becomes a teenager. "How do you know?" I asked him out of curiosity. "I just know," he responded, with a sound of confidence in his voice that put me to shame. The truth is, I *do* know that my older son loves me. He has always loved me. But days with unrequited hugs are hard. Thankfully, the lesson they teach hasn't been wasted on me.

These discouraging and lonely days are nothing that my Heavenly Father hasn't experienced Himself countless number of times before *because of me*. Never again will I forget how much my Heavenly Father needs those moments of attention and affection that I neglect to give Him, for one reason or another. This is what I tell myself, and this is what I intend to do. But no sooner have I declared it than I hear a voice inside my heart telling me something different. *Without a doubt, you will forget again, My child.* I don't like these words of the Future-Teller. I don't like this about myself! "But I don't want to hurt You, God," I protest with all of the sincerity I can muster. ***I know***, the Still Small Voice whispers back. *Just as your own child doesn't want to hurt you....*

Chapter Thirty-Four

THERE'S ONLY ONE PERSON WHO CAN REALLY HELP YOU

"SINCE GOD CHOSE YOU TO BE THE HOLY PEOPLE HE LOVES, YOU MUST CLOTHE YOURSELVES WITH TENDERHEARTED MERCY, KINDNESS, HUMILITY, GENTLENESS, AND PATIENCE. MAKE ALLOWANCE FOR EACH OTHER'S FAULTS AND FORGIVE ANYONE WHO OFFENDS YOU. REMEMBER, THE LORD FORGAVE YOU, SO YOU MUST FORGIVE OTHERS. ABOVE ALL, CLOTHE YOURSELVES WITH LOVE, WHICH BINDS US ALL TOGETHER IN PERFECT HARMONY." COLOSSIANS 3:12-14 NLT

I'd been his physician for a few years, and he had always seemed so easy-going. To tell you the truth, his wife was the one who had intimidated me (though a doctor isn't supposed to admit such things). While Mr. Heal* had kept things simple and was always polite, Mrs. Heal had sometimes made me feel like I was walking on eggshells. There had been her memorable calls to the answering service and the messages which typically insinuated that I was ignoring one or more of her husband's important—and potentially life-threatening—medical problems. These were not to be outdone by her requests to be put on speakerphone during her husband's clinic visits. "My wife wants to be on the phone and listen. Is that alright?" he would ask dutifully, with an almost apologetic tone. "Sure. No problem," I would respond out loud, with a smile on my face, though my heart would always sink a little because I knew that a visit that would normally have only taken twenty minutes (and been virtually complaint-free) was now going to take twice as long and feel more like a job interview.

In spite of my personal feelings about her involvement, it was obviously a positive sign for Mr. Heal. It told me that she loved her husband of three decades and didn't want him to die—or even to suffer with the symptoms of a non-life-threatening disease any more than he had to. One of the saddest things I hear in clinic is that a patient has no one in the entire world to accompany them and drive them home from the colonoscopy I have recommended. "No one at all?" I typically ask in surprise, while trying not to make them feel any worse. "*No one,*" they reiterate without hesitation.

At least Mr. Heal had someone—and not just anyone. He had an *advocate*. Actually, he had two advocates, because his step-daughter seemed to be a clone of his wife. Involved. Assertive. Defensive, when she thought that Mr. Heal was somehow being neglected. She'd even been the one to call the clinic while he was still hospitalized to report something involving his inpatient care by other physicians that she had concerns about.

One day, Mr. Heal contracted pneumonia and ended up in the hospital. Thankfully, he made his way back home within a week, albeit with a new home oxygen requirement that he wasn't too pleased about. As is the custom following a hospitalization, he came to see me for a follow-up visit.

Mrs. Heal accompanied him, of course, as I assumed that she would. I took a deep breath and headed to the waiting room to get them, bracing myself for the usual inquisition with every step. Relief washed over me when Mrs. Heal smiled and appeared to be in a good mood. As we walked back to my exam room, I felt more optimistic than usual that Mr. Heal's visit would be straightforward.

I could've never prepared myself for what was actually about to happen instead. We made the usual small talk and then dug into the details of the hospitalization itself. Aside from his new metal sidekick—the oxygen tank that he was now unhappily tethered to—Mr. Heal seemed no worse for the wear. I was just about to examine him with my stethoscope when he made an unusual statement. "I'm in trouble," he announced, with a tone that I couldn't quite decipher at first.

Seconds later, the mystery began to unfold as Mrs. Heal told the story of a different marriage than the picture I had painted in my mind since the very beginning. "He's not very nice. He's even *mean*." I was truly surprised by her revelation but managed not to change the expression on my face. "Don't get me wrong," she continued. He's not physically abusive. "Although, you did push me out of the way at the bottom of the stairs this morning," she said as she remembered the events from earlier in the day and shifted her glance from my eyes to those of her husband. "She wants me to leave and go stay with my brother in Iowa* for a while, but I don't know what good that would do," Mr. Heal suddenly announced.

"How long have things been like this?" I asked, as I wondered if the pneumonia itself may have been a stressor that triggered a mood or personality change that was now causing the disharmony. Mrs. Heal's response told me differently. "For most of our marriage—though not in the beginning or I wouldn't have married him," she clarified. "He's a Curmudgeon," she then summarized, before attempting to apologize in her own way.

169

"I know this isn't a therapy session...." "It's okay," I nodded, to let her know that it was alright to continue, as I thought back to another patient's recent stories about his daughter's attempt to get advice regarding his grandson's problems. "These are *behavioral* issues," she was told repeatedly by the pediatrician, who clearly wanted to make it known that behavioral issues were not within her scope of medical practice—or responsibility. Normally, I wouldn't have had any extra time to spend on social issues during a hospital follow-up visit either, but Mr. Heal was my last patient of the day. And although I still had a lot of after-clinic work to do, I could sense that they needed this time far more than I did.

Mrs. Heal began to weave a story together that told me that the disharmony in the home wasn't only affecting their marriage. It was impacting every family member in the home, including his stepson, daughter-in-law, and little granddaughter. And his stepson, in particular, was grieving the loss of the relationship they'd once had.

Next, she spoke about her own hurt, and I began to see her in a whole new light. "You're so nice to everyone but your family. When you were teaching that teenage girl how to drive the 4-wheeler*, you were so patient with her. But when it was me—and I made the exact same mistakes that she did—you yelled at *me*." Her eyes made their way back toward mine. "He loves our little granddaughter, Harper*, and she adores him. But even she asks sometimes, 'Why is Grandpa so mean to you?'"

I knew that Mrs. Heal was hoping I would have a solution for the biggest problem that she had ever laid at my feet—and I *really* wished that I did, too. But I actually had no idea what I could say or do that was going to make things better. Because I didn't want Mr. Heal to think that I thought less of him now—or to feel like our visit had been used solely to vilify him—I gave him the opportunity to share his side of the story. He didn't deny the things his wife had accused him of, which surprised me. Neither did he excuse his behavior. The truth is, even he didn't know why he was taking his family for granted or pushing away the very ones he loved the most.

As I listened to his own stories, it became apparent to me that Mr. Heal viewed and handled nearly every situation differently than his wife and children did. Their personalities and ideas about life were polar opposites. And it was taking its toll and causing them to retreat into their own caves of frustration, anger, hurt, and loneliness. "Have you gotten any marriage counseling?" I asked, assuming that they probably hadn't. "Yes, we did," Mrs. Heal answered, almost immediately. "It didn't make any difference," she summarized. *Hmmm*, I thought, as I processed her unexpected response. *Now what*?

Maybe they just needed to be reminded of the famous mantra and morbid reality that today is all we are given. I told them a couple of true stories that came to mind: a man who said sadly at his wife's funeral, "I loved her so much, I almost told her once," and a ninety-year-old patient of mine whose wife told him she loved him for the very first time just one week before she alone knew that she was going to die. "I know that the four of you love each other," I said, with a tone of certainty, referring to both them and their adult children at home.

The unhappy pair was silent but didn't disagree, so I continued. "How do you want to be remembered at your funeral?" I finally asked, as I turned and looked Mr. Heal directly in the eye. "What do we want people to remember and be able to say about us?" I asked next, in summary of the only thing that really matters for any of us in the end. I could tell by the expression on his face that he wanted to be remembered positively. (Who doesn't?) Mr. Heal clearly wanted to be known for the *real* feelings that he held in his heart but couldn't seem to show. Yet there was another look on his face that conveyed the defeat that he had already resigned himself to.

In my mind, I quickly ran through every possible tool I could think of that might fix the problem. *What can I offer him?* I asked myself over and over again, hoping that my brain would be able to come up with a brilliant solution (or any solution at all, frankly). I had seen certain medications help the irritability of patients who'd been given these prescriptions for other reasons. Usually, it was a serotonin-boosting drug that I would ask about when I saw it on the medication list of a new patient. "Is this for depression or anxiety?" I typically ask for clarification of their medical history. "Neither one," they sometimes say. "I take it so I don't yell at my husband or bite my kid's head off," one woman explained. "It's my anti-jerk pill," another man said. (Or perhaps he used a different word with a similar meaning that wouldn't be appropriate for this book.)

My eyes scanned Mr. Heal's current list of medications and then stopped when I saw it. He was already taking a medication that increases the availability of serotonin, the happy, calming chemical of our brains—and the dose wasn't low either. For a moment, I could feel the disappointment in my heart *physically* somehow. But Mr. and Mrs. Heal were oblivious and didn't yet know that I had nothing left to offer them. I knew that I was going to have to tell them this within the next few minutes, and it's the part of the job that every doctor dreads.

As I opened my mouth to relay the bad news, a thought suddenly came into my head. There was someone who could help, after all. It wasn't me or the wonders of modern medicine. It wasn't psychology or the marriage counseling that had already failed them. But there *was* hope—and in leading them to it, I simply had to know where I was starting from. "Do you have any spiritual or religious background?" I asked cautiously. "We go to church sometimes," Mrs. Heal answered first.

And with that, I walked through the door that I now understood was open ever so slightly. "There's only one person who can really help you," I said, with a certainty that I knew to be true. The expression on their faces changed in an instant—just as the feeling of helplessness in my heart did. I couldn't tell you exactly what I said next, because the words weren't mine, and I don't even remember them anymore. What I *can* tell you is that I brought them to the Great Physician—the One who can heal relationships as skillfully as He can heal physical diseases.

In Christ's presence, attitudes change—and the self-interest that we all harbor within our hearts miraculously melts away. With the gift of His own precious example comes patience for one another and the ability to see our own role in the development of our broken relationships where we couldn't see it before. And for those relationships that are estranged through no fault of our own—to bring us peace—He is able to fill our hearts with forgiveness when we are unable to do it on our own. Sometimes, this forgiveness leads to the restoration of a relationship that is still in the best interest of both members. Other times, this forgiveness serves to dampen the pain from a lost relationship that can never be fully healed on this side of Heaven.

For the husband and wife of thirty years who were sitting before me—and the family at home that they represented—reconciliation appeared to be something they both craved. They simply didn't know how to get there. Relationships are fragile on this sinful planet of ours, and no amount of counseling and serotonin is going to fix that for all of us. In the eyes of Mr. and Mrs. Heal, I could see that frustration and hopelessness were already beginning to lose their grip.

But I knew that they needed something more, and I pondered this as I picked up my stethoscope and proceeded to listen to Mr. Heal's heart and lungs. I checked his legs for swelling next, as I mustered up the courage to ask the most important question yet. "Would it be alright if I prayed with you before you go?" I watched as a look of relief washed over their faces almost immediately. "I would love that," Mrs. Heal responded without hesitation, as both she and Mr. Heal moved closer to the place where I was standing in the middle of the exam room.

We naturally formed a small circle, and I put my arms around each of them, as I asked the Holy Spirit silently to give me the words to pray. Out loud, I asked Jesus to heal this family and to continue to wrap His arms around them and give them patience and understanding for each member—even when it feels much easier to go back to the way things were before. I prayed that they would find a support system at their church that will continue to encourage them in His name. As the prayer ended and we opened our eyes, I saw them smile for the first time that day.

They had arrived with a storm in their hearts and a sense of defeat, but they didn't leave that way. Counseling hadn't been able to put the pieces of their marriage and family back together again, just as medication had not. They had laid their most pressing problem at the feet of an earthly physician. And although she could often heal hearts physically—and could sometimes heal them emotionally—she was powerless to heal them from the disease of sin that is our greatest threat of all. Yet, because of Jesus and Jesus alone, they felt lighter and airier as they said goodbye to the physician who'd had no solutions of human design left to offer them but somehow felt like she was walking on cloud nine. And within their hearts was a priceless hope that had previously eluded them.

*Names and some details changed to protect the privacy of my patient

Chapter Thirty-Five

THE FBI

"If you openly declare that Jesus is Lord and believe in your heart that God raised him from the dead, you will be saved." Romans 10:9 NLT

The first time I met him, I naturally assumed that he had once worked for *the* FBI. Never before had I seen those letters without thinking about the Federal Bureau of Investigation of our United States of America. And many of the Veterans I've doctored have had unique and impressive careers following their years of military service, so a retirement from the FBI wasn't out of the realm of possibility in my mind. It wasn't until I got closer to Mr. Faith* that I could see the real meaning of those three capital letters on his hat. The fine print on his red FBI baseball cap read: Firm Believer In Jesus.

As a fellow believer, I appreciated the boldness of his faith from the very beginning of our relationship. Eventually, it became his hallmark. Each time I saw him for our biannual clinic visits, he was wearing that FBI hat proudly like a crown—but not for his own glory. Whether it made him look cool to some or like a fool to others didn't seem to matter, and I admired that about him. He wasn't a closet Christian and could never be accused of being ashamed of the gospel.

Beyond that, the label of Christian wasn't false advertising in his case, as it sometimes can be. I'll never forget the day that my long-time patient from Tennessee—who knew that I'm a Christian and whose own world view had led him to teeter between atheism and agnosticism—told me that his "Christian" boss was known for treating his employees badly and had recently yelled at his wife on the phone right in front of him. I literally winced as he shared the story. Sadly, it would have been better for Christ's reputation if this man had kept his religious affiliation to himself. It was a cautionary tale that reminded me that I must constantly be aware of how *my own* words and actions at work may color my co-workers' views of the Jesus I claim to follow.

With Mr. Faith, there was never a time when his opinions or behavior seemed to be at odds with his identity as a follower of Christ, whether it was with me, the nurses, or the administrative staff. (Like Santa, the doctor hears *all*.) What you saw was what you got, with Mr. Faith. And this usually involved a contagious smile and easy-going attitude. Although there were plenty of things to complain about on the problem list in his chart, he was bothered by very little. This was the essence of the man in the red FBI ball cap. *This* is what I remembered when I received the unexpected news that COVID-19 had stolen the rest of his life.

Mr. Faith had been vaccinated with a single Johnson & Johnson vaccine seven months prior to his death—just one month shy of the recommendations from the CDC and FDA that a booster be obtained six months after the first dose. Without complaining, he had worn his mask. He had done what he could, but it wasn't enough. He sought help at a local hospital and took all of the medications that were ordered for him. When the supplemental oxygen wasn't enough, he accepted the BiPAP therapy

176

that was offered to him next—but he continued to struggle and gasp for air. Finally, when it was time to decide whether or not he wanted to be intubated, sedated, and put on a ventilator—with no guarantee that he would ever come home—Mr. Faith chose the palliative care and comfort measures that had also been offered to him.

No doubt, he knew where he will spend eternity when he wakes up from death at the longed-for resurrection. After all, he Firmly Believed In the One who made this possible in the first place—his true friend, Jesus Christ. Mr. Faith had no immediate family to remember him after he was gone. No spouse. No children. No living siblings. And if not for the red FBI baseball cap, he may not have stood out to me from my panel of 1200 patients either. But this Firm Believer In Jesus will forever be etched into my memory now. Ultimately, he made the *only* choice in this life that actually matters for eternity. Rest well, my fellow FBI Jesus friend. Rest well until we meet again, and your famous red hat has been replaced with the crown you'll say you don't deserve.

*Name changed to protect the privacy of my patient

CHAPTER THIRTY-SIX

THE TATTERED KINGDOM

"IN THE TIME OF THOSE KINGS, THE GOD OF HEAVEN WILL SET UP A KINGDOM THAT WILL NEVER BE DESTROYED, NOR WILL IT BE LEFT TO ANOTHER PEOPLE. IT WILL CRUSH ALL THOSE KINGDOMS AND BRING THEM TO AN END, BUT IT WILL ITSELF ENDURE FOREVER." DANIEL 2:44 NIV

It was supposed to be the stronger flag. At least that's what they promised. The sun, wind, rain, and snow were supposed to be no match for its strength and durability. And oh boy, did it look *amazing* waving back and forth majestically in the land of the free on my new twenty-five-foot, hurricane-proof, aluminum flag pole. Breathtaking she was! The Stars and Stripes. Old Glory. Red, White & Blue. America the Beautiful. How proud I am to be an American—most of the time....

I can remember feeling this pride even as a child. "You live in the best country in the world," I was told, as far back as my memories will take me. And the greatest proof of this bold claim is the fact that millions of people from all over the world long to become citizens of my United States of America, too. From the ends of the earth, the reputation of my beloved country has been one of coveted freedom, plenty, and limitless opportunity—not to mention power and success.

The outward evidence of my love and allegiance to the country that has blessed me was obvious. In the 8th grade—just one year after the Berlin Wall had fallen—I played Lee Greenwood's song, "God Bless the U.S.A."[1] incessantly, as it made its big come back during the Gulf War that year. My heart swooned as I listened to those words: "And I'm proud to be an American, where at least I know I'm free. And I won't forget the men who died, who gave that right to me." Sometimes, I even sang along.

Then in the summer of my 10th grade year, there were the jean shorts that looked as if they'd been cut straight from an American flag. Hands down, they were my favorite piece of clothing. I wore them patriotically everywhere shorts were actually considered to be an acceptable form of apparel. (Where'd you go, beloved flag shorts?)

I felt so lucky to have been born in the United States of America out of *every* country on this planet. Occasionally, I also felt guilty about my great fortune when I thought about the lives of the people who'd been randomly born into poor, third world countries—or the nations that lock their citizens in prisons of total control. I wondered what even my ancestors from better countries than these had thought when they made the decision to head for America—like my great-great-grandfather, Christian Olson Herum, who got on a boat because he believed that 19th century life in Norway wasn't as good as it would be here. I thought that nothing could ever dampen my love for the country I prized.

But the years passed, and I grew up. Before I knew it, I was a tax-paying, working adult who watched the news and had finally become aware that politics existed. I drifted from one political party to another and began to hear of congressional decisions that flew in the face of common sense and seemed to be driven by the politicians' party lines, donors, and desire to be re-elected. As the disappointing and unexpected reality set in—suddenly, I didn't feel so proud to be an American anymore.

I continued to have birthdays and so did my country. This was the one constant in both of our histories, whether they were emotionally entwined or not. Time marched on. As I became even older, I watched in confusion as some took our America for granted and put her down with words or actions that they were only allowed to say and do because she had given them that very freedom in the first place. It was things like this that brought my country back to my heart.

The older, wiser me was finally able to see things as they really are. This country of mine—and the Congress that makes her decisions—is made up of sinful humans, just like me. Even when we are at our best and most altruistic, it will be impossible for us to run a kingdom the way that God does. Sinless, just, and merciful, He is—not only part of the time, but at every moment. The God of Heaven is perfect in wisdom, yet full of love—a combination of traits that is so very rare in our world. I realized that it had been unrealistic for me to expect *any* earthly kingdom to be everything I wanted it to be—even a country that was built on such idealistic principles as mine.

With this in mind, out came the flags once again. First came the large wooden American flag from Hobby Lobby that has hung on the walls of three different homes now. Next came the wooden firecrackers and tray that were painted in the Star-Spangled Banner and scored on Etsy. Then came the flagpole that has proudly flown the American flag on our current property for at least a quarter of a century. The faded flag of the previous owners was replaced with a new one as soon as we moved in.

And when the locks of the telescoping mechanism began to fail, the original white pole with its quirky leaning posture was uprooted from its cement anchor and replaced with a stronger, taller, black version. It only seemed fitting that the heftier pole be paired with the highest quality flag possible. So, that's exactly what I sought and hung in my yard to show the world my gratitude for the imperfect country that was unable fulfill all of my expectations but has still given me the best and most coveted gift of all—**freedom**.

Unexpectedly, the new pole proved to be capable of hanging two flags, rather than a single flag, like the old pole could. Immediately, I thought of the Christian flag that displays the same red, white and blue colors in a unique pattern and ratio all of its own. I thought about hanging this particular flag above Old Glory, since the kingdom of Jesus is undoubtedly superior to even the greatest of earthy empires. But I was told by a knowledgeable and well-meaning friend that American flag etiquette decrees that The Stars and Stripes must always take the first position.

I found my own Christian flag easily enough on Amazon. Its colors were crisp, and it seemed to be sturdy—although the company's description had made no claims of its weather-proof nature or longevity like the seller of the American flag had. I hung it beneath my country's flag as tradition instructed and immediately began to enjoy the beautiful scene. There's just something about a flag flying high above you as the unseen wind entices her to dance with him gracefully. And I was lucky enough to have *two* of them.

Nine months and three seasons passed. Each time I pulled into my driveway, I was greeted by the flags that stood as tall as my rooftop—and almost appeared to be waving at me as they welcomed me home. It was a beautiful, picturesque scene that never got old. But much sooner-than-expected, one of those flags *did* get old.

The first time I noticed it, I couldn't believe my eyes. One of my cherished flags was torn in multiple spots, while the other flag remained intact. From there, the deterioration was surprisingly rapid. Like the sock that didn't get a stitch in time, this particular flag soon needed nine. It split in ways I never thought were possible—not only horizontally but vertically, along the edge of the flag that hugged the pole. Soon, this particular rip allowed the entire flag to get caught on the pole in a manner I'd never seen before. Along the outer edge of the flag, the horizontal tears grew in record time.

And the worn, raggedy flag stood in stark contrast to the perfect flag *beneath* her—an obvious metaphor of a bigger truth I couldn't miss. Two flags representing two kingdoms, only one of which will last. The tattered kingdom of the Stars and Stripes and the indestructible kingdom of the Cross.

Chapter Thirty-Seven

A Terminal Diagnosis

"Inasmuch then as the children have partaken of flesh and blood, He Himself likewise shared in the same that through death He might destroy him who had the power of death, that is, the devil, and release those who through fear of death were all their lifetime subject to bondage." Hebrews 2:14-15 NKJV

It was the summer before my second year of medical school when my older sister Heidi was given the heartbreaking news. Her beloved dog, a Bichon Frise she'd named Tango Monet, had been diagnosed with a disease whose manifestations and unavoidable outcome could only be described as tragic: disseminated Granulomatous meningomyeloencephalitis or GME. In spite of the treatment with steroids that he was offered, the veterinarian had declared that little Tango would be dead within a couple of months. Naturally, Heidi was devastated.

It seemed like just yesterday that my sister had brought him home from the breeder as a puppy, after convincing our parents that she needed a canine companion before she headed out to California to start medical school. Only two summers earlier, the always-smiling Tango Monet had arrived at our Nashville home following his adoption. Heidi began the *daunting task* of training her new friend—a description that seemed fitting from my vantage point. Our bedrooms were right next to each other, and the walls were apparently thinner than they looked. Years later, my ears can still remember the sleepless nights of barking . . . and barking . . . and barking.

I hadn't brought home my first newborn yet, but I was quite certain that this Bichon puppy's sleepless nights were reminiscent of the sleep schedule of a human baby—only instead of middle-of-the-night feedings and diaper changes, there were repeated trips to the toilet of the great outdoors. And though I felt most sorry for my sister, I was still frustrated by the repeated interruption of my own sleep. I hadn't signed up for this, as she had, and I dreamed of the day when Heidi's puppy would finally sleep through the night. Eventually, he did—just as babies always do, although it truly feels like you will *never* sleep again before that happens.

The next two years with Tango were wonderful for my sister. He settled into the new apartment they shared with Heidi's medical school classmate, Marisol, and her African gray parrot Elvis. Like all Bichons Frises, my canine nephew was known for his Bichon Buzz: a comedy show in which he would get riled up and run around the room, jumping from one piece of furniture to the next and spinning around in circles before finally collapsing. Tango Monet was always happy and full of energy—until one day, he wasn't.

When he was only two years old—still just a young teenager of fourteen even by dog years—Tango's body began to fail him. First came the vomiting of whole pieces of his dinner shortly after each meal. Next came the obvious visual impairment that would cause him to walk into walls. A short time later, he couldn't even walk at all. X-rays showed that his esophagus was massively enlarged and unable to function because the cranial nerves from his brain stem were no longer able to signal it. It was these same damaged cranial nerves that could no longer help him to see—or even hear normally. Worst of all, the neurons in his brain and spinal cord were too inflamed to allow him to move. But, why?

What triggers the inflammation of the nervous system in cases of GME? A viral or bacterial infection? A type of cancer? No one really knows. But for all of the unlucky fur-patients, their body's own immune system appears to be involved. Confused and suddenly unable to correctly differentiate between self and non-self, the rogue immune cells of the victim begin to attack the brain and spinal cord, as if it were a foreign invader that must be destroyed. And destroy the dog's nervous system it does.

While it is painful to see any living being suffer, it's especially difficult to stand by and watch helplessly as the most innocent patients go through things that they cannot even understand. For animals, babies, and those with special needs or dementia, there is an extra layer of fear that the rest of us don't have to experience. Unable to communicate—or grasp the meaning of our words even if they could—they are left to feel their bodies betraying them without explanation . . . or hope. *This* is what I worried about as I watched the control center of young Tango's body shut down rapidly in ways he couldn't possibly comprehend.

A terminal diagnosis had been given, and the clock began to countdown the weeks until the grave would claim dear Tango Monet. Prednisone was prescribed by the veterinarian in order to make him more comfortable and buy my sister's best friend a little bit more time. But Heidi had been given no false hope. The outcome of her beloved dog's cruel and sudden illness was certain, and the fact that the veterinarian had declared it so could be clearly seen on my sister's face each time I saw her. Ever visible on the outside was her heart's inward heaviness.

Yet there was a mission of distraction that was fairly clear. In order for Tango to survive even a few months more, he would need to eat. But how? Without a working signal from his inflamed cranial nerves, his enlarged and weakened esophagus was now unable to do what it was made to do—squeeze each bite downward in the direction of the stomach below, so that it would not come back up after he swallowed. This, the veterinarian knew too, and he gave my sister the best advice that he could.

From that point on, Tango's food would have to consist of wet dog food that had been carefully rolled into small balls. Meatballs for every meal. *Weighty* meatballs that gravity could pull down into his stomach without effort, since his esophagus obviously couldn't assist. But who would make sure that the fur-patient remained in a gravity-friendly position for thirty minutes after each meal?

As a medical student who was transitioning from the third to fourth year of training, my sister didn't have the luxury of a summer break like the ones we remember so fondly from our earlier years of student life. The very last summer break for a physician-to-be comes between their first and second years of medical school. So, Heidi's sick best friend was going to need a caretaker, and it obviously couldn't be her. Call it luck or call it Providence. I had just finished my first year of medical school.

That summer of 2000, it was me and Tango "Pango" Monet, as I affectionately called my fur nephew (because the extra, rhyming middle name was just so fun to say). Early each morning, I allowed my alarm clock to pull me out of my comfortable bed, so that I could be at my sister's apartment to dog-sit before she had to leave for the hospital. The patient wasn't able to greet me at the door the way he used to, but he was aware of each arrival nonetheless. Our days consisted of scheduled meals, timed bathroom breaks, and candid conversations in front of the television. Of course, there was cuddling involved.

Though he was still potty-trained and not incontinent either, Tango was fully dependent on his caregivers to get him to his outdoor bathroom. Thousands of times before, those four furry little legs had bounded down the stairs and *run* back up again. But suddenly, they couldn't, and he didn't know why. "Why won't you move, legs?" his eyes seemed to ask as I announced each bathroom break, and his body remained uncharacteristically still. Those same eyes would then clearly say, "thank you," each time I carried his limp body back up the stairs into the air-conditioned apartment.

Mealtimes were different, too. For breakfast and lunch each summer day, I prepared the lone menu item of meatballs, making sure that each one was perfectly round and just the right size. But this wasn't the most important job I had. Creating weighty meatballs that gravity could pull into the stomach wouldn't be enough to overcome the damage to Tango's esophagus that his neurological disease had caused. This gravity that he needed actually had to be harnessed manually.

So, just as the veterinarian had instructed, I held my canine friend in a vertical, upright position for thirty minutes following each meal—all in the hopes that each meatball would make it through his enlarged and paralyzed esophagus. Although he was too weak to wriggle in my arms or even think about escaping, I still knew that this particular position wasn't one he was accustomed to. I had only seen him standing on his hind legs before when food was at stake—and even then, he stood for just the second or two that it took to snatch the pizza crust or coveted treat that he'd been eyeing. But I was determined that Tango "Pango" Monet was going to eat.

The days passed—each one a carbon copy of the others, with all of its predictable rituals. Naturally, I bonded with the sweet and helpless animal in my care. And somehow, I got it into my head that there was actually an alternative to just sitting around and waiting for him to die. A large, framed picture on my sister's living room wall had caught my eye. Within this print by painter Nathan Greene, a scene of encouragement was depicted in which Jesus stood behind a perplexed physician who was sitting at his desk and pondering "The Difficult Case" before him. A large medical textbook lay open in front of him, but I knew that if the portrayal in front of me bore any resemblance to the truth of real life, it was the hand of The Great Physician on the doctor's left shoulder that would ultimately give him the wisdom he needed to heal his patient.

Although I knew that the portrait on the wall had no special healing powers of its own, I couldn't help but bring him there. Frail and doomed to die, Tango Monet had nothing else to lose. Like the paraplegic man in Luke Chapter 5, my furry new friend couldn't get to Jesus on his own—and so I carried him. Technically, I laid a Bichon Frise on some carpet in front of a picture on the wall. Symbolically, I laid a beloved dog with no chance of long-term survival at the feet of Jesus Himself.

But my attempts to help my sister's best friend went beyond symbolism. Ultimately, prayer was the biggest weapon I had against the fatal disease that had already claimed Tango's future. And I prayed *hard* for that sick little dog, as I knelt over him below that picture of the Great Healer. I told Jesus that I was certain that He cared for Tango, since He knows when a sparrow—worth far less—has fallen (Matt. 10:29-31). "The human veterinarian can't heal him, but *You* can," I declared with confidence. "I know that You hate to watch him suffer even more than I do. All You would have to do is lay Your hand on him, and he would be well again." Day after day, I laid my terminally ill patient beneath the picture of Jesus and prayed this same heartfelt prayer.

This wasn't the first time that I had reached out to Jesus on behalf of a fallen family pet. My thoughts drifted back to the fall of 1986. The news of the family cat's death had come while we were on our annual Columbus Day week-end trip to Vermont. Normally such a happy time, the vacation had been marred by tears for the loss of 13-year-old Frosty, who had been under the care of a pet sitter in our brief absence. The steroids Tango was taking for meningomyeloencephalitis hadn't been enough to save Frosty from the ITP or idiopathic thrombocytopenic purpura that he'd been fighting, and he had gone to the grave. Not quite ten years old at the time, I had actually asked my friend Jesus to raise Frosty from the dead—and believed that perhaps, He would.

Not even the twenty-three-year-old me who was praying with such bold faith now would have ever believed that God would answer such a prayer. But the nine-and-a-half-year-old child version of myself certainly had. The adults out there can probably already guess that the answer to that particular prayer of mine was no—and also understand the reasons for that. Eventually, I did too. Even so, I imagine that Heaven was actually tempted to reward the unusual faith of that child back in October of 1986 as she prayed so earnestly by the secret garden grave of a white Persian cat whose 2.7 billion base pair genetic code God had already memorized and planned to re-create one day.

And as the Prince of Heaven listened to the prayer of a dark-haired girl for the family cat that she had lost, He wrapped His arms around her to comfort her. "I know that it won't make sense to you right now, but it would not be the best thing for Me to answer your prayer in the way that you are hoping I will." These words the Gentle Healer whispered to her heart. And her heart heard them. What she could *not* hear were the words that He spoke next. *One day, Child, when you're all grown up, you'll ask Me to spare your sister's dog, Tango, from an early death. And I will say yes.*

You will ask me to give him more years of life, but you won't expect the number of extra years that I will grant him, nor will you presume that I will restore him to perfect health. Yet, I will answer your prayer beyond your wildest imagination. Fifteen more years I will add to his life because of your faith and persistent prayer—fifteen years, like King Hezekiah (2 Kings 20:6). And there will be no trace left of the cruel disease that will devastate his nervous system when he is two years old—and was otherwise destined to take his life. For I won't just spare his life, I will re-create it.

The years passed, and life unfolded just as the Future Teller predicted that it would. A Bichon Frise puppy was born and adopted by a woman named Heidi who loved him instantly and called him Tango. After two glorious years together, he suddenly became severely ill with a rare disease that shut down his nervous system and promised to pull him into an early grave. But the woman's sister heard the inner voice of the Heavenly Healer, and it changed everything. "Ask Me to save his life. Bring him to Me, and ask me to make him well. Tell me that you know I see each sparrow fall, so you're certain that I care for dogs, too." So, ask Him, she did. And the doors of the grave were shut to keep Death from a beloved two-year-old Bichon named Tango Monet. Miraculously, his nervous system was fully restored, and he lived a long, healthy, and completely steroid-free life until it was time for him to say goodbye at the ripe old age of seventeen.

I don't know why God answered this particular prayer of mine. Some of you may be wondering the same thing, because you once prayed whole-heartedly for the life of your *human* family member, yet they still died. Was my sister's dog more important than your loved one? Or, did I simply pray harder than you? Undoubtedly, the answer to both of these questions is *no*.

Only a year later, God would say no to me, too, though I prayed just as fervently for another life (which is a story for another chapter). All I know is that a dog who was declared to be terminally ill by his earthly doctor became completely well after he was laid at the feet of Jesus. And Heaven knew that I would write the story now. It's a story that tells us a lot about Jesus, but don't miss the most important part of all.

As incredible as it is to know that the Creator of the Universe sees each sparrow fall and was willing to heal a dying dog in the summer of 2000–just because someone He loves was bold enough to ask—He wants to do so **much more**. We are *all* terminally ill from the disease of sin, and without a Savior to rescue us from the clutches of Death, there is simply no hope for any of us. Fifteen years later, Death came for Tango a second time. And this time, he was allowed to take him—just as Death ultimately took King Hezekiah and was able to reclaim Lazarus and the daughter of Jairus. Death will inevitably come to take us, too.

This would be the sad ending of the story—with Sin and Satan being forever victorious—if not for the turn of events they never saw coming. The Son of God Himself submitted to Death, so that He would have the right to free us from it. Redeemed from Death through the death of a righteous and perfect Savior—*that* can be our legacy, if only we will choose it.

CHAPTER THIRTY-EIGHT

THE JOB MOMENTS

"IN ALL THIS YOU GREATLY REJOICE, THOUGH NOW FOR A LITTLE WHILE YOU MAY HAVE HAD TO SUFFER GRIEF IN ALL KINDS OF TRIALS. THESE HAVE COME SO THAT THE PROVEN GENUINENESS OF YOUR FAITH—OF GREATER WORTH THAN GOLD, WHICH PERISHES EVEN THOUGH REFINED BY FIRE—MAY RESULT IN PRAISE, GLORY AND HONOR WHEN JESUS CHRIST IS REVEALED." 1 PETER 1:6-7 38:4 NIV

I never imagined how hard it would be for me to have a baby. And I certainly never dreamed that I would ever get mad at God and give Him the silent treatment. Yet, both of these things are part of my story. If I'm going to tell it, I must tell it honestly—for although the ending was a happy one, the lesson of a spiritual lifetime was hidden in the middle of the dark days that came beforehand. If I hadn't actually experienced it, I would never believe that the things I'm about to write about could take place in my heart (neither the good, nor the bad). But clearly, I needed to know....

If it was possible to close the book on these painful memories and never think of them again, there's a part of me that would do it without a moment's hesitation. Another part of me, however, knows that this would be selfish—and perhaps even unwise. As is the case with many things in life, I believe that this experience was meant to be shared for the benefit of others. And I don't dare forget it, or else I would put myself at risk of forgetting my blessings and repeating my mistakes. So, I'll re-live it for you—and I'll re-live it for me—before it goes back in the vault.

I've always wanted to be a mother. Even now, memories of treasured times spent role-playing with Cabbage Patch dolls come flooding back. Years later, I can still remember the name of my first preemie Cabbage Patch doll—Daphne Clarice. She had the coolest pacifier and a single tuft of yellow (yarn) hair on top of her otherwise bald baby head. On occasion, I convinced my younger brother, Heath, to play dad with me. We would dress the Cabbage Patch dolls with the baby clothes we had once worn ourselves (which our mother couldn't part with yet).

After my Mom fought massive lines at the mall to bring my babies home in the 1980s, my wish list didn't stop there. I wanted everything that a real baby might need: a high chair, carrier, and stroller (no doubt influenced by the advertising company for Coleco Industries). Lucky for me, each Cabbage Patch accessory eventually made its way to my home. I dreamt that one day, it would all be real.

When I married Jason in the middle of my first year of medical school, I didn't plan on having kids right away, but it actually had nothing to do with the fact that I was a busy graduate student. I simply figured that we would enjoy being a twosome for a few years. The Baby Bug had his own ideas, however, and bit me just months after we said, "I do." Try as I might, I couldn't rid myself of the baby fever he'd infected me with. There was no turning back.

I told my husband that I wanted to stop taking my birth control pills, just so that I could be ready for later. "It can take a while for the cycles to return to normal after a woman stops the pill," I explained. And although this is technically true, I didn't actually think that it would happen to me. My Jason had *not* been bitten by the Baby Bug (yet), but ever the easygoing one, he at least found it within himself to humor me.

So, the birth control pills went into the trash, and I pretended to be nonchalant about the future. Yet inside, I was anything but relaxed and took note of each day and week on the calendar. *Months* passed. Still no return of the cycles that the pills had previously been tasked to suppress. At the six-month mark, I still blamed the prior oral contraceptive use, although the Internet claimed that delayed and irregular menstrual cycles from previous birth control pill use would only last up to six months. "Lies," I said out loud to the computer monitor, as if the authors of these references could actually hear me (because I still didn't realize the truth).

Eventually, some version of my former periods returned, but they weren't the same. I hardly recognized them. Future research centered on finding other women whose fertility had been affected by birth control pills long after they were stopped. Like most things we search for on the internet, I was able to find what I was looking for. There were stories of at least a few cases similar to mine. But mostly, I was alone in my strange and unwanted experience.

One day, I found a book called "Taking Charge of Your Fertility," by Toni Weschler, MPH.[1] The author knew what she was talking about and opened my eyes to many facts about female anatomy & physiology that aren't taught in medical school, just as she claimed. Armed only with an inexpensive basal body thermometer—and without any costly lab work—I was able to determine that I wasn't ovulating. It had now been nine months since I had ditched the birth control pills, and my future plans for the birth of a baby were still very much being controlled. For the first time in my life, my body wasn't doing what it was supposed to for an extended period of time, and there was no end in sight—until the day it appeared that there might be.

Finally, that first morning temperature began to rise. After ten months (that had felt even longer), it was clear that at last my ovaries had woken up from their hibernation. This would've been enough to encourage me. But as I continued to plot each morning's basal body temperature on my old-fashioned graph paper, I became even more excited because that temperature rise just kept on going. According to Toni Weschler's book, eighteen consecutive higher temperatures is a telltale sign of pregnancy (with few exceptions). As I looked at the latest chart in front of me, I couldn't believe my eyes. I was *pregnant*.

A couple of positive pregnancy tests later, and it was official. I had conceived the very first time that I actually ovulated. I was cautiously optimistic, knowing that anyone can have a miscarriage. (And the odds aren't exactly what I would call low at 15 to 20% of pregnancies.) My time was split between allowing myself to think about a future with the baby that was growing inside me and telling myself not to get my hopes up or dwell on anything pregnancy-related until at least the second trimester. The limbo did not last long.

On Valentine's Day, as Jason and I returned to our apartment with plans to order pizza (following our failed attempts to find a restaurant that didn't have a two to three hour wait for couples without a reservation), the holiday of love became a night of heartbreak instead. I started spotting and knew that it was bad news. Even the positive stories on the Internet were unable to encourage me. Instead of a restaurant—or even the consolation prize of a pizza delivery—our Valentine's date was spent in the emergency room. I simply had to know the truth about what was happening inside my uterus before I could fall asleep that night or show up to class the following morning.

The staff at my medical school's own emergency room seemed sympathetic enough, but I didn't care for the cardinal rule of radiology technician behavior that I learned about firsthand during my experience as a patient: *never* reveal to the patient what you're seeing on the screen. Although I would meet other radiology techs years later who were willing to bend the rules, this particular ultrasound technician followed them strictly. Like the soldiers who guard the Tomb of the Unknown Soldier in the Arlington National Cemetery, she remained stoic and never spoke—except for the moment when she replied to my question about her findings with, "You'll have to wait for the doctor to tell you."

A couple of days later, the obstetrician that I was meeting for the very first time under less than happy circumstances didn't mince words. Although she did so kindly, this doctor told it like it was and didn't leave me with any false hope. There was a heartbeat, but it was slow, and the baby also measured small for my dates—at least a week behind. Both of these things were signs of a pregnancy in jeopardy, and for the second time in two days, I left a medical facility with a diagnosis of *threatened miscarriage*.

Although I was careful to keep my guard up in order to protect my heart, the presence of a heartbeat—even a slow one in a poorly growing baby—still left the door open for hope. So, I walked on through it and did what I'd been taught to do when the storms come. I prayed. Beyond that, I sought the support of women who knew what it felt like to walk in my shoes—and I thought that I had found them. In particular, I had stumbled upon a website that appeared to be exactly what I needed as a Christian—a group of fellow believers who had prayed for the healing of their threatened little unborn babies and *won*.

The peril surrounding my tiny baby was understood, but I was oblivious to the even greater danger that now surrounded me as I embraced the seemingly-innocent version of Bible truth this apparently trustworthy group of believers promised. If you pray hard enough—and your faith is big enough—your threatened miscarriage will stop. And your baby will ultimately live. Bible verses were shared that were said to provide the assurance—and even the guarantee—that I needed:

- "Ask and it will be given to you...." (Matthew 7:7 NIV)

- "Therefore I tell you, whatever you ask for in prayer, believe that you have received it, and it will be yours." (Mark 11:24 NIV)

- "If you have faith as small as a mustard seed, you can say to this mulberry tree, 'Be uprooted and planted in the sea,' and it will obey you." (Luke 17:6 NIV)

I had hope! Hard work and persistence have always been my forte. And my faith was even *bigger* than a mustard seed. So, it seemed to me that if the words of Jesus were true—and I believed that they were—then the outcome of my prayer request was certain. This troubled pregnancy of mine would have a happy ending, if only I prayed and believed.

One day, I shared all of this with my sister, Heidi—threatened miscarriage website promises and all—and the look on her face took me by surprise and shook my confidence. Before she even spoke, I knew that she didn't agree with my assumptions. I wanted to believe that this was simply because she had less faith than I did, but I knew that she is a fellow Christian who accepts the existence of miracles and answered prayers. I'll never forget what she said, although I certainly didn't like it. After making sure I knew that she hoped the answer to my prayer would be the one I wanted, she tried to prepare me for the opposite possibility. And then she added the most memorable part: "God is not a genie lamp."

Perhaps God used my sister to prepare me for the unwanted answer He knew was coming. But it didn't hurt any less when I learned that His answer was no. After two weeks of an emotionally painful limbo, the miscarriage that had been threatened finally occurred, and the tiny baby I had very much wanted was gone. My heart hurt, of course, but my head hurt more. Why hadn't the promises of Jesus that I'd clung to proven to be true?

I didn't know it yet, but I was about to spiral down into a spiritual crisis that I'd never thought was possible for me. It wasn't the first time that God hadn't answered one of my prayers the way I'd wanted. It wasn't even the first time that He had said no to something that was really important to me. It was, however, the first time that I had specifically claimed the words of Jesus in faith—the ones with no apparent caveats—and they had returned to me empty. It felt like I'd been lied to.

Why had Jesus made these promises in the first place? He certainly didn't have to because He doesn't owe us anything. But since He had, it seemed to me that He should honor them. In my quest for answers that would be able to salvage my weakening trust in the Father and Son, I sought the advice of others.

My first stop on this journey was to revisit the threatened miscarriage website that had promised victory through prayer. I don't know what kind of response I was expecting, but it definitely wasn't the one I got. Perhaps, there was a brief token condolence, but I don't remember there being any genuine empathy. What I will never forget is the message that was conveyed in reply to the news of my particular unwanted outcome. *I must not have prayed hard enough, or if I had, then my faith wasn't as strong as it needed to be instead.*

What this told me was that God's help wasn't truly a gift, because it had to be earned with a different kind of currency—an A grade on my prayer of faith. Apparently, the creator of this supposedly Bible-based threatened miscarriage support group had gotten a different, happier answer from God than I did. And she credited herself for asking in a way that evidently, I had not. Her prayers were obviously superior to mine based on our differing outcomes, and that was that.

I continued to go to church, but the message seemed to be the same. God will always fight for you when you pray. The older senior pastor of the church that held my membership gave a sermon one Sabbath that especially upset me. He spoke about a battle in the Old Testament in which God gave the Israelites a huge victory. They had been far outnumbered and had inferior weaponry, but God showed up—and suddenly the odds didn't matter. As he tried to encourage his parishioners, this pastor worded his sermon in a way that sounded awfully familiar to the rhetoric from the threatened miscarriage website.

Ask God for help, and you cannot lose the battle you're fighting. His wording left no room for any other possibility. And I could feel the anger welling up inside my heart. Was he arrogant enough to presume that God would never say no to *him*? Or was he simply naive because *he'd* never suffered a significant loss after pleading with God for help?

All I knew was that I couldn't stay. So I left in the middle of the message that day, husband in tow. Still, I didn't think about leaving for good. I called up the church office to ask for some pastoral counseling, and a meeting was arranged for me with the younger associate pastor. As the story spilled out, he was undoubtedly sympathetic but unable to provide any real answers.

I asked the young pastor point-blank if he had ever experienced suffering *personally*. He shared that he'd been diagnosed with leukemia as a baby and then acknowledged that he didn't remember it, so the suffering was really his mother's instead. And, of course, this suffering—and the prayers his mother no doubt prayed—had a happy ending. I left that meeting feeling no better than I had before. But at least he hadn't insinuated that my prayers weren't good enough (like the creator of the threatened miscarriage website had), and I appreciated that.

My next stop was to pay a visit to the hospital chaplain who had been teaching my Christian medical school's Bible class. Ironically, we were studying suffering and the book of Job. My instructor showed empathy—and didn't pretend to have all of the answers I needed. And although he was much older than the associate pastor I had talked with before him, he had also been lucky enough not to have experienced any significant losses in his life.

Knowing this, he didn't pretend to know how I felt. So instead, he shared an article about a father who had lost his wife and three children in a car accident. It was written by the father himself, and his faith had survived the nightmare. I admired him, of course. Obviously, my loss paled in comparison to his, and I knew it.

There was actually never a moment when I thought that my suffering was especially great or unusual. Women have miscarriages, and it doesn't even happen infrequently. It wasn't that I thought God should spare me from all of life's bad luck either. Why should misfortune only happen to someone else? Why *shouldn't* it happen to me? That's the profound question that the father who'd lost his entire family had asked. And I understood what he meant even then, although it was a lesson I had only just learned.

With this in mind, I want to reiterate that my beef with God wasn't that He had allowed something bad to happen to me—it was that this bad thing happened to me *after* I had specifically asked Him for help because of a promise His Son had made. Had I experienced a bigger loss *quickly*, so that there had been no time to beg for His help beforehand, I wouldn't have felt that He had failed to keep His word. This line of reasoning can be picked apart, of course, but it's what I told myself at the time.

With my trust in God at an all-time low, I stopped talking to Him completely for the first time in my life. It was a foreign thing to me. I had been the girl who preached sermons to her stuffed animals as a 6-year-old about how God can use even children to share His message. In high school, college, and medical school, I had prayed for God's wisdom and help each time I sat down to study—not only when it was time to take the tests. I had found comfort in the fact that He could see the future I couldn't, when my heart was broken in high school by my first love. God had always been there for me, and He had always proven to be right each time He had said no before. But suddenly, our lines of communication went silent.

Months passed, and in the midst of the valley between Heaven and me that *I had created*, there was an emptiness that I had never felt before. And the timing couldn't have been worse, because after the miscarriage came a long period of infertility that made me feel even more broken than I already did. The loss of a baby was difficult enough to experience, and I hadn't imagined that things could get worse, but they did. Typically, the one consolation following a miscarriage that most women have is the knowledge that they can try again, and that prospect had initially given me hope. All too soon, however, that solace was taken from me as well, for I stopped ovulating completely.

I sought help from the OB/GYN who had treated me for my miscarriage, Dr. Gaio. "Making a human being is an intricate process that can be hard," she had once told me. And as I looked around in rooms filled with hundreds of people, I couldn't help but wonder how it was possible that their mothers had birthed them so easily, when it seemed so impossible for me to make just one human. Dr. Gaio prescribed a medication called Clomid for me, and I finally ovulated. But as each cycle passed without a positive pregnancy test, I ovulated later and later in spite of taking higher doses of Clomid.

As Murphy's Law would have it, it was time for my OB/GYN rotation in the third year of medical school, and most of the month was spent in the hospital with pregnant patients. I can still remember one day, in particular, when I was tasked to help deliver a baby. Normally, this would've excited me, as it does most medical students. But for me, it only brought heartache, and I spent time in the bathroom wiping tears from my eyes and splashing my face with cold water in the hopes that no one would know I'd been c rying.

The basic duty of attending church was also daunting at times. Jason and I had transferred our membership to the church that was on the campus of my medical school, after I decided that I could no longer listen to the senior pastor at our old church following the sermon that had felt tone deaf to my particular spiritual crisis. I still couldn't pray, yet I didn't feel ready to leave the church behind completely. So, each week I continued to show up. Most of the time, it was bearable. But sometimes, it wasn't. And on those Sabbaths, I had to walk out for my own sanity—like the day the service was dedicated to mothers. Thankfully, my tenderhearted husband left with me, and I never had to explain the reason for my departure.

As the days passed, I continued to put one foot in front of the other. Yet I felt helpless to make my body do this most basic thing that the majority of women have to take birth control just to prevent. For most of my life, I had been able to get what I wanted simply by working hard enough. Now it felt like I was stuck in a ditch that no amount of sweat and toil could accomplish my escape from. Each month felt longer than the one before it, and there seemed to be no end in sight to the identity of infertility that I had never dreamt would become mine.

Then one day as we flew home to see my parents for vacation, the unexpected happened. As was my custom, I sat in the window seat of the plane and opened the shade so I could view the world in ways that I am never able to see it from the ground. It still amazes me each time I watch the buildings and cars below appear to shrink and become the size of tiny toys, while the plane ascends higher and higher, surpassing even the clouds. On this particular day, the experience began no differently.

But something changed inside my heart and mind as I flew above the clouds and thought of the words of God to Job when it has been his turn to question God's fairness. Had I been the one to stretch out the sky and create the heavens? No, I'm essentially the size of an ant on the ground below instead, unable to reach even the firmament without an airplane. The skies that I hadn't made looked utterly *glorious*—and I was humbled in that moment. Who was I to tell the One who had given me the ability to think in the first place that I had declared Him untrustworthy? Who was I to tell the Creator of promises that He had broken one?

After a full year of the silent treatment, I finally prayed again. I don't remember any of the words I said, but I will never forget that God listened and never made me feel any less worthy to be his child this time around. Undoubtedly, I had been a prodigal daughter of sorts. And He was clearly reminiscent of the father in the parable from Luke chapter 15–watching and waiting anxiously for my return while I was still far off. My circumstances hadn't changed, but my outlook had. The heavy monkey of infertility was still on my back, but I felt lighter and airier.

Eventually, I decided to consult with a reproductive endocrinologist (aka "fertility specialist"). I had begun to think that I might have polycystic ovarian syndrome or PCOS, and I let him know about the many cysts that had been seen on my ovaries on the ultrasound Dr. Gaio had performed. "Those aren't specific to PCOS," he told me. "Any woman who isn't ovulating can have the same findings on ultrasound."

As a medical student, I had come to associate PCOS with an overweight, "bearded lady." This was the disease's poster girl, after all—and undoubtedly, my fertility doctor had learned the same stereotypes. "You aren't overweight," he thought out loud (although I had recently learned that as many as half of women with PCOS aren't). "You don't have excess hair," he continued, in an attempt to explain why I probably didn't have PCOS. (I actually *do* have hirsutism or extra hair that I pride myself on removing as most women with it do, but he never asked.) Lastly, he looked at my neck and said, "You don't have acanthosis nigricans either"—the velvety brown skin discoloration that comes from insulin resistance (which only three percent of women with polycystic ovarian syndrome actually have on exam).

The options for infertility treatment that I was left with were costly and came with no guarantees. I was discouraged, of course. And then came the conversation with my father that changed everything. An internal medicine physician like I, too, would become one day, he knew a thing or two—and as luck would have it, he had recently listened to a Continuing Medical Education lecture about polycystic ovarian syndrome by Audio Digest. My Dad didn't need to ask if I had extra hair because he already knew me so well. "You clearly have PCOS," he declared without hesitation.

And then he did something about it. Although I don't have diabetes, my father prescribed a first-line diabetes medication called metformin for me. Within two months of starting the metformin, I ovulated on my own without the help of the drug Clomid that had recently been failing me. Even more exciting was the discovery that came next. I was *pregnant*.

I was cautiously optimistic—at least when I considered that the statistics were in my favor. The odds of having *two* miscarriages in a row were reassuringly low. I didn't take this for granted, however. Every single day—multiple times each day—I prayed for the survival of this baby. Several weeks passed, and it was finally time for my first OB visit—the standard 10-week checkup. With my heart in my throat, I met with Dr. Gaio and told her how nervous I was to get the ultrasound that was planned. She asked if there had been any spotting this time, and when I said no, she told me that I had nothing to worry about.

As the ultrasound commenced, I looked away at first. When Dr. Gaio didn't say anything after a couple of minutes, I turned my head so that I could watch her face. I noticed what *wasn't* there first. There was no smile. Dr. Gaio remained silent as her face studied the monitor, her brow somewhat furrowed. I looked at the monitor too and saw my baby. Why wasn't she saying anything? I had the distinct feeling that she was stalling. "Is everything okay?" I finally dared to ask. At last, Dr. Gaio looked me in the eye, and I could see the tears. "I can't find a heartbeat," she managed to tell me. My baby also measured two weeks behind in size.

The next couple of hours were a blur—both literally and figuratively. I couldn't see, because the tears wouldn't stop and clouded my vision. Dr. Gaio sent me and Jason over to the hospital radiology department for another ultrasound to confirm her diagnosis of a "missed miscarriage," because she didn't want to schedule a D&C to end the pregnancy until she was certain that my baby had really died two weeks earlier, as it appeared. I sat in the full radiology waiting room—with a very pregnant woman in front of me—and sobbed out loud. Although I was annoyed with myself for crying publicly, I couldn't make it stop. When it was finally my turn, I closed my eyes during the second ultrasound that I had no illusions would show anything different.

I spent the next day in bed, still technically pregnant but no longer pregnant with any hope or purpose. Sweet Jason called out of work to be by my side and comfort me. Sometimes, he tried to make me laugh and turned movies on to provide a distraction. Other times, he held me in silence and didn't make me talk at all. Still other times, he cried with me.

Somehow, my husband made that long day of limbo and sorrow seem bearable. And when the next morning sunrise finally came, we drove to the hospital to end the pregnancy that we had both wanted so much. When I awoke from the anesthesia, my sister's med school roommate, Marisol—now an anesthesiology resident—was there and told me that she was sorry for my loss. In response, I could only weep. I was unpregnant once more.

At the starting line all over again—and without any promise of ever finishing the race—it hadn't escaped me that I had a decision to make. It wasn't a choice between trying to become a mother or giving up on my dream, for I knew that I would never quit until there was a baby in my arms. The determination I had to make instead was about my God. Would I judge Him to be untrustworthy now, as I had the last time that He had chosen not to grant the wish I'd prayed for with all of my heart? Or would I prove to be faithful this time, instead, and show Him that I meant what I'd said in that airplane far above the horizon?

An opinion about God was mine to make only because *He* had given me the free will to do so in the first place. And I am happy to report that in this re-do I hadn't wanted, I clung to God and never actually considered leaving Him again for even a moment. I would never tell you that God caused my baby to die, or that He needed to find out whether or not I would stand by Him this time—for He already knew what I would do. But *I needed to know*. I needed to know if I was capable of remaining loyal to God in the middle of the trials—when I didn't get the answer to my prayer that I wanted.

I've always felt a bit sorry for the resource officer who ran and hid during the mass shooting at the high school in Parkland, Florida.[2] It's much easier to shame him and be angry, of course, because it's likely that fewer teenagers would've died had he been braver and willing to risk his life for theirs. But I have also thought of things from his perspective. No doubt, he has shamed himself and will never be able to wash away the guilt and embarrassment that now undoubtedly plague him. Perhaps he even rewinds the video of that day—that can never be erased from his mind—and then imagines an edited version of those moments in which he becomes a hero, rather than a coward.

Almost certainly, he had never imagined that he would abandon his post on that horrible day and had previously lived with a different assumption about his valor. None of us want to find out that we lack courage when the real-life test comes. And this man will now be stuck with that knowledge forever—unless, of course, chance grants him an unlikely do-over.

My own second chance was the one consolation that I had in the midst of this newest all-too-familiar period of grief. Although I hadn't wanted to lose again, it was the only way I could find out for myself that I love God for who He is—and not only for what He can do for me. "I trust You," I told Him, although He had told me no. *Again.* This time, I let God comfort me—instead of blaming Him and running away—and I could literally feel His arms around me as I sat in the medical school lecture hall, with another pregnant classmate just two rows in front of me. No longer tied to a particular outcome, my hope was solely dependent on God this time around.

I made this decision without the promise of a baby. The only guarantee I had from God was that He would never leave me—as I had once left

Him—and it was enough. Finally, I realized that I didn't want a God that I could control (even with His own promises), just as I didn't actually want to live in a world where I could assume that those who are suffering simply hadn't prayed as well as I had. These were the lessons I learned in the valleys that I would never have been able to learn from the hills. And I'm so glad that I learned them before it was too late, for I couldn't have known that just eleven months later, I would hold my firstborn child in my arms.

CHAPTER THIRTY-NINE

THE WILIEST WEEDS

"BUT WHILE HIS MEN WERE SLEEPING, HIS ENEMY CAME AND SEWED WEEDS AMONG THE WHEAT, AND LEFT." MATTHEW 13:25 NASB

W eeds are a pet peeve of mine. In fact, I think it's fair to say that I actually *hate* them. I couldn't tell you exactly when my loathing of weeds began. Perhaps our contemptuous relationship was born when I became a homeowner for the first time. Or maybe it developed the day that I could no longer remain oblivious to their ostentatious presence in my yard. All I know is that I've got a lot to say about weeds, and they have *got* to go.

Like any formidable opponent, the weeds of my displeasure have never gone quietly. Even if they're technically incapable of making noise, they sure do know how to bring it out of me when we do battle. And do battle we must.

There are multiple tools available to the person who wants to extricate the weeds from their mulch—and I say *mulch* because the word garden is probably a stretch for what I've accomplished in the landscaping department, if I'm being honest. (I've learned that I'm much better at keeping people alive than plants, after all.) Classic weapons in the war against weeds have long included herbicides (AKA plant poisons) and various weeding devices bearing proprietary names that'll instantly give you the confidence you need to fight the toughest opponents. My husband has added a blow torch to his own weed-killing arsenal, while some farmers are now using newer electrocution techniques. (I don't know whether to be fascinated or scared by either of these tactical maneuvers.)

Personally, I prefer to use my hands. I typically find myself being drawn into these battles at the most random and inopportune times so that putting on gloves is the farthest thing from my mind. As a result, these barehanded fist fights are always dirty and have even been known to draw blood. Most often the weed is the loser, and the sweat involved is minimal—as long as I don't let the weeds go unchecked for too long. A memory living within the storage house of negative reinforcements inside my brain dutifully ensures that I will never forget this.

I can still see it now: the appearance of lush green foliage in the distance. The sight actually looked pretty from the vantage point of my mailbox at the end of the driveway—especially considering the fact that winter had just recently ended and not much vegetation had survived the freezing temperatures. But as I approached the walkway to my front door on that particular spring day, I discovered a far different reality. This bed of green consisted *solely* of weeds—too many different kinds of weeds to count. Smooth, skinny weeds and coarse, thick weeds. Short weeds and tall weeds. Weeds with shallow roots and weeds with deep roots. There were even weeds with razor blades! Now *that* was a mulch battle I never want to find myself in the middle of again.

And this whole problem with weeds has got me thinking about spiritual things. There is an obvious analogy that I can't help but make between two natural occurrences that I continue to find myself in conflict with over and over again. Yet the connection I'm about to make may not be the one that first comes to mind when you think about menacing weeds and important spiritual matters because the 13th chapter of Matthew contains a famous parable you're likely familiar with—and it makes a different type of association. In verses 24 through 30, an enemy purposely plants weeds in the wheat fields of the King of Heaven, and Jesus later explains in verses 36 through 43 that the weeds represent a group of people (those who will ultimately choose another kingdom in the end).

It turns out that weeds make pretty good metaphors. In the parable of my mind, there's a garden that's truly worthy of the name, unlike the strategically located zones of mulch with sparse offerings of eye-catching plant life that surround *my* house. Every part of this garden is significant, even—and *especially*—the weeds.

The soil is my life—a blank slate with all of its unique opportunities and personal choices. I can use the soil to grow beautiful flowers, bushes, and trees—or leave it bare instead. If I do choose to plant, I can sow a little or sow a lot. I can select seeds that grow easily and become flowers that thrive in any environment, or I can pick seeds that require a lot of work to nurture. Regardless of what I decide, however, *something* is going to grow in this dirt. And the less I pay attention to my garden, the less I will like what it becomes. For I've leaned that the weeds grow without any effort at all.

It's the beautiful things I'm most proud of and want others to see, such as the soft, pink rose petals and charming, yellow daffodils that represent the good character and deeds of kindness for which I want to be remembered. If I could simply speak my analogy into existence, my life's garden would look just like the flower shows my father used to take me to as a child. But alas, both my literal and figurative canvases of mulch look nothing like that piece of botanical artistry—not even close.

I've already confessed that there is more mulch than greenery in my yard. But technically, that's only true if we're talking about *intentionally* grown plant life because weeds are green too, after all. Most often though, I'm compelled to pull the weeds out as soon as I see them. It doesn't matter if I'm heading out the door to go to work—or even running late. If one of those pet peeves of mine catches my eye, these hands are going to get dirty. I simply cannot help myself. The compulsion to rid my property of an ugly, uninvited weed is *strong*.

So why aren't I as vigilant about removing the weeds in my spiritual life as I am about the ones in my yard? Why do I pull out the physical weeds by their roots quickly while allowing the tares in my soul to stay and grow? These are rhetorical questions I believe I already have the answer to, although this knowledge doesn't actually make it any easier to live with my obvious double-standard. And that's probably because the stakes are infinitely higher.

Maybe my unequal treatment of the weeds in the spiritual realm is at least partly due to the fact that they're less obvious. Sure, some weeds are easy to spot, such as boldly broken commandments. Who doesn't know when they're lying as a child—or that they've just taken God's name in vain? Other intangible weeds are more difficult to discern. We are admittedly less likely to realize, for example, that we're breaking the tenth commandment when we want the life that someone else has—or that we're breaking the fifth commandment when we treat our parents with less respect than they deserve. Then, there are the incognito weeds that inevitably gain height and strength before they're even on our radar, because they're not among the Ten Commandments at all—things that aren't inherently bad but have the potential to slowly choke out our connection to God when we prioritize them over time with Him. (You know what I'm talking about.)

These metaphysical weeds are undoubtedly tricky. It isn't merely that they're harder to see. The crux of the matter is that they're more difficult to uproot. And sometimes we don't actually *want* to let them go. That's not an easy thing to admit to myself, but it's the truth. There are weeds in the spiritual world that I don't hate—weeds that I'm actually fond of. These ethereal weeds come in many forms, but their end result is the same: *I am separated from God.*

The apostle Paul's honest words of vulnerability come to mind. "I have discovered this principle of life—that when I want to do what is right, I inevitably do what is wrong. I love God's law with all my heart. But there is another power within me that is at war with my mind. This power makes me a slave to the sin that is still within me" (Romans 7:21-23 NLT). It all seems pretty hopeless—these weeds that inevitably make their way into our hearts—and I think it's time for another confession.

There is a weed in my yard that I haven't removed. One day, I simply discovered a giant weed I couldn't pull. I tried, of course, but it wouldn't budge. Its stalk was huge—*is* huge, since it's still in my mulch. This weed I cannot wield has gotten the better of me. And the most concerning part is this: I don't even remember seeing it when it was smaller.

There's a lesson for me here, I know. This invasive plant simply came and made itself king of my yard without warning—and I can't uproot it. That *scares* me. The longer this thing lives, the more tightly it clings to the soil beneath the surface and becomes part of my property. Clearly, I need a gardener who is better at weeding than I am. I need a horticulture hero! But right now, things aren't looking very good for me in my battle with this deeply entrenched weed, and it's no different with my spiritual garden.

Without a savior, this story—*our* story—is undoubtedly going to end badly. I think Paul put it best in Romans when he said, "Oh, what a miserable person I am! Who will free me from this life that is dominated by sin and death?" (7:24 NLT). And if that's all there was to say, our future wouldn't be worth talking about. But our Heavenly Father provided a solution, and Paul begins the good news with praise. "Thank God! The answer is in Jesus Christ our Lord...." (Romans 7:25). The wiliest weeds are no match for this rescue team.

CHAPTER FORTY

THE ABSOLUTE AVENGER

"FOR HE HAS RESCUED US FROM THE KINGDOM OF DARKNESS AND TRANSFERRED US INTO THE KINGDOM OF HIS DEAR SON, WHO PURCHASED OUR FREEDOM AND FORGAVE OUR SINS." COLOSSIANS 1:13-14 NLT

We Americans love our superheroes. Whether it's the Marvel characters like Iron Man and Spider-Man, as my kids prefer, or the DC Comics characters like Superman or Batman that my husband favors instead, we adore our superheroes. We look up to them for their bravery and courage. We exalt them for their strength, smarts, and special powers. We admire them because they are simultaneously cool and humble. And we *especially* esteem them for saving the world from the evil villains.

With few exceptions (because I would never presume that there wouldn't be on our sinful planet), we root for the good guys. We cringe when they're being lied about by the enemy, and the lies stick. We want to cover our eyes when the bad guy is pummeling the good guy, and it appears that they—and injustice—have won. Injustice is something that none of us want to accept, even when our view about what constitutes justice in a particular case is the polar opposite of our neighbor's. While injustice prevails, we feel unsettled, sad, and even angry. We wish that there was something we could do to make things right, and when there isn't—and we feel helpless and hopeless—we yearn for a rescuer. We need our very own superhero. If only the movies we attend in droves were actually real.

As I write this, I can still feel the emotions that last night's Spider-Man movie[1] elicited in the hearts of a room full of people, including mine. Just days earlier, the film had made a box office record to become the third-best opening of all time—making $253 million in one weekend. And which movies hold first and second place in cinematic box office history, you ask? Two other Marvel movies—Avengers: Infinity Wars[2] and Avengers: Endgame.[3] We *love* our superheroes.

The signs of our infatuation are everywhere. Giant movie posters hang on the walls of our theaters and houses. The faces of our superheroes are imprinted on clothing designed for all ages at our favorite stores, and we wear them proudly like badges of homage. We find them on our children's toothbrushes and tubes of toothpaste. Need some additional reminders of the champion you favor? A key chain? A Christmas tree ornament? A backpack? Sheets for your bed? A watch? A bobblehead doll? You can find it on Amazon, eBay, or Etsy, I am certain (not that I shop at these stores ridiculously often or anything). Even as I write this, my eight-year-old son is discussing his plans to spend his Christmas money on a Spider-Man costume—full bodysuit, face mask, web launching gloves, and all. If only the cherished guardians behind these replicas really existed.

What if I told you that all of the superheroes that Hollywood has ever dreamed up *combined* can't even come close to the splendor of a real-life Superhero? Would you be surprised? Could you be convinced? For those of you who already believe in Jesus, have you ever thought of Him this way? Sit back and relax while I present to you the greatest superhero story that has ever been told. (The following fairy tale was inspired by the Bible, my favorite authors—Ellen G. White and Graham Maxwell—and my imagination.)

* * * * * *

Once upon a time, there was an enchanted kingdom called Bliss. Its benevolent King was a beloved and immortal creator deity named Elohim (El-oh-heem). He reigned with love and perfect justice, and his dynasty was a paradise, where his subjects—the beautiful seraphim—wanted for nothing and had never known sadness, fatigue, sickness, pain, or death. His rules were few and did not feel burdensome. King Elohim's son Prince Michael was equally revered. He was brilliant and strong—yet equally kind and humble—and the inhabitants of Bliss couldn't help but want to be near him.[4]

Third place in power and popularity was Daystar, the kingdom's choirmaster. More charming and handsome than any other seraph in Bliss, he was ever surrounded by admirers. Every member of the kingdom looked up to him and trusted him implicitly. Daystar had been named for his dazzling personality and appearance. He lit up every room and garden that he entered. But he was known for more than his friendliness and good looks. He was also wise and full of good advice, frequently mentoring the people of Bliss in the ways that an older brother or pastor would. And because he often had the ears of King Elohim and Prince Michael—who had bestowed him with such an honor—his council was valued even more.

As time passed, an unexpected and peculiar thing happened in the kingdom of Bliss. Within the heart of Daystar developed an emotion that had never existed before. Pride. The beauty and brains that King Elohim had generously and lavishly created him with begot pride. (Ezekiel 28:17) And that pride begot jealously—jealousy of King Elohim and jealousy of his son, Prince Michael, the very ones who had gifted him with his glamour, talents, and esteemed position in the first place. Forgetting that he wasn't a deity as they were, Daystar felt that he had done so much for the king—and been so close to him—that he should at least be equal in power to his son. The distinction that King Elohim placed between them began to hurt his feelings and sow discontent within his heart.

In the beginning, this novel feeling of jealousy was only the size of a tiny seed, so no one could have ever imagined that it would nearly destroy the entire kingdom. As the seed that had taken root in the heart of Daystar grew, he exalted himself and began to believe that *he should be a deity, too*, and sit on the throne like King Elohim and Prince Michael—to be worshipped as a god by those who had already adored him as an anointed leader of his fellow created beings. And forgetting that even his very breath is continually dependent on the life-givers he was now strangely and arrogantly rebelling against, he began to sow his seed of discontent inside the hearts of his fellow citizens of Bliss. Using the intellect that the deities he now deemed his enemies had graciously given him, he concluded that there was only one way to succeed at his hubris-driven mission of treason. If he was going to become a god and sit on the throne, he would need the support of as many of the inhabitants of the kingdom as possible.

This change in loyalty wasn't going to be achieved easily, however, for Daystar knew that the citizens of Bliss loved the royal father and son above all others. If he was going to have any hope of swaying the hearts of their devoted followers, he must first weaken the trust between them. But how? Not only had King Elohim given them everything they needed, he had also given them everything that they could possibly want—things they hadn't even known existed before he gave these gifts of his creation to them freely. The seraphim of Bliss were truly happy—and beyond that, they knew that they were each loved by King Elohim intimately, as if they were the only one in the land. It was this love that especially drew them in and caused them to praise the king continually. He knew that he could never reveal to them that his true motive for seeking the throne was for his own gratification.

Daystar thought back to the days when *he* was filled with spontaneous praise for King Elohim, too. "What was it that first made me stop trusting him?" he asked himself, as he tried to remember. The truth is that **he needed a reason not to trust** in order to justify his rebellion of pride to the citizens of Bliss—and even himself.[5] And so, his mind created one. "He tried to keep me from being free," Daystar finally said out loud to no one but himself (for now). "*This* will be the key," he thought silently, just as a sly smiled formed on his lips. "We *all* want to be free."

Without delay, Daystar—the bright star and darling of the kingdom—set out to position himself above King Elohim and Prince Michael. He was especially jealous of the king's son, whom he felt was no more worthy of honor and power than he was.[6] "I am like god, after all—and just as exceptional and praiseworthy as Michael," he told himself. (Isaiah 14:12-14) "So why shouldn't I use my abilities for more important tasks than the ones the king has given me? My talents and beauty are truly being wasted. I was made to do so much more!" And the right-hand man of Bliss's royal deity family took the first step towards treason within his heart, when he convinced himself that it would all be for the good of the kingdom.

"Let me try it on *one* citizen first," Daystar decided, just as an advertising agency would test a small focus group of potential buyers initially, before spending the big dollars on a commercial that might not effectively sell their product. Nervous excitement filled the pit of his stomach as he approached one of his biggest fans. "Have you ever wondered what it would feel like to be *free*?" he asked his closest friend, Gable, who looked surprised.

"Free?" Gable repeated aloud, with a tone of confusion in his voice, as he pondered the seemingly innocent question that his beloved choirmaster and long-time companion had posed. Regardless of the conclusion that Gable might draw, he couldn't possibly know how important his understanding of the truth would become.

Ultimately, Gable answered Daystar's inquiry with his own question. "Don't you *already* feel free?" Daystar shook his head side to side for effect as he carefully prepared his rebuttal. "How can I feel free—how can *we* feel free—when King Elohim has given us a list of commands that we must follow?"[7] He watched Gable's face intently as he attempted to make his case more convincing. "We are wise enough to know what's best for us, and unless we're given the right to make our own decisions, we can never truly be happy." Daystar could see that his friend was pondering his claims with some reluctance. "But King Elohim *loves* us," Gable finally responded. "Why would he ask us not to do something, unless it was truly for our own good?"

Daystar could feel himself becoming annoyed with his friend—and what he felt was his naivety—for the very first time. And for the very first time, Gable also heard a tone in his beloved mentor's voice that made him feel something he had never experienced before. He didn't even know what to call it, but it didn't feel good. And he had *always* felt good before.

It was becoming apparent to Daystar that it wouldn't be as easy as he thought to weaken the citizens' trust in King Elohim. But he wasn't done trying. "The king created us with brilliant minds and his very own wisdom, and we can be trusted to make good decisions on our own, Gable. His commands aren't necessary to keep us safe. They are only for him—to highlight *his* power and keep us under his thumb."

Daystar took a breath and then plowed through the remainder of his speech—which he made up as he went along. "You only feel free because you didn't know why the commands were made. But I discovered the king's real intent as I spent more time with him and Prince Michael. You know that I am with them more than anyone else. How could you be expected to know the truth from afar? That's why I'm sharing it with you now and couldn't keep it to myself—because you're my best friend, and I thought that you deserved to know. I love you enough to want true freedom for you, too."

Gable felt an uncomfortable knot in the pit of his stomach as he realized at that very moment that things would never be the same—no matter whose side he chose. "I'll think about what you've said, friend," he replied to Daystar, putting his hand on his mentor's shoulder before walking away. Daystar himself began to feel a bit uneasy in his heart. If he couldn't convince the friend who looked up to him most, perhaps his quest to become king was going to be harder than he thought—but, surely not impossible, he told himself. He was confident that he would be able to gain the loyalty of enough of the citizens to take the throne. "I'm worthy of it, too," he said out loud this time, though no one was around to hear it.

A voice inside Daystar's head—the conscience that hadn't yet been fully silenced—whispered its warning. *You don't have to do this. It's not too late to go back to the way things were before. Just tell Gable that you thought about what he said and realized you were wrong. He'll be more than happy to forget that it ever happened.* For a moment, this thought seemed wise, and the unsettled feeling that had recently taken residence within his heart seemed to diminish.

But then, his pride began to speak more loudly than his con-science—and this was the voice that he preferred. So, he listened more intently. *The things you said to Gable about King Elohim weren't just a ploy to undermine his trust in the royal father and son, so that you can be king.*

They're actually true. It isn't right for King Elohim and Prince Michael to restrict our liberties. The citizens of Bliss need you to be the god of freedom.

As Daystar's inner voice continued to ration his plot, the more convinced he became that his plans were justified. *How can it be treason when it's for the good of the seraphim?* he reasoned. *They only believe they're happy under the reign of King Elohim now because they don't yet realize what I have already figured out—that his commandments have bound us all with invisible chains. For me to awaken them and enlighten them with the truth would be a gift.*

With new resolve, Daystar set out to build his army of followers.[8] And though Gable ultimately proved not to be one of them—remaining loyal to King Elohim and Prince Michael instead—Daystar was still able to convince one-third of the citizens of Bliss that they would be better off with **him** as their leader. For some, it was his promise of true freedom that bought him their loyalty, while for others, it was simply his claim that he loved them more than the royal deity father and son did, which ultimately gained him their allegiance. For all of them, his charismatic personality, perfect beauty, and captivating speeches drew them in and persuaded them to rebel against the ones who had created them and given them everything.

And there was war in Bliss. (Revelation 12:7) Prince Michael and those who remained devoted to King Elohim fought against Daystar and those who had defected in pursuit of a freedom that they were led to believe was being kept from them unjustly. The mutineers fought hard but ultimately lost the battle and were expelled from Bliss permanently. (Revelation 12:8-9) Although the winners and losers of the Battle for Bliss had been forever decided, life on *both* sides of the kingdom's gates was never the same.

Outside the gates, the rebels tried to adjust to a dark new normal they could've never imagined—and wished with every fiber of their being that it was merely a nightmare they would eventually wake up from. The followers of Daystar—who became known as Diablo after his failed coup—were not of one mind when it came to their ideas about his culpability for their misfortune. To some of them, he was still a hero, who had merely been unable to overcome the larger, more powerful army of the deity king that wanted to control them. To others, he was the smooth talker who had duped them out of paradise forever. Still others asked themselves, "What am I supposed to believe *now*?"

Inside the gates, there was no joy for the victory the loyalists had won. Instead, somber expressions replaced the once carefree countenances of the citizens who were left behind as they struggled to understand how so many of their friends could have lost their way. An unfamiliar feeling of loneliness washed over them each time they saw the empty chairs that had once been occupied by the lost one-third. (Revelation 12:3-4) "Why did you do it?" they cried aloud, although they knew that the exiles couldn't actually hear them and probably wouldn't even know the answer to this question themselves even if they could.

King Elohim and Prince Michael had won the battle, but this knowledge couldn't heal the wounds that Diablo's betrayal had inflicted on their hearts. Contrary to what Diablo had claimed, their greatest desire was **love**—*not* power, although power had always been an inherent part of who they were. Their commands had been expressly made to protect their citizens from harm, and it hurt deeply to know that Diablo had used the existence of these rules of love to vilify them. It didn't matter that they still had complete authority, riches, and glory. There was an ache in their hearts that cut deeply each time they thought about Diablo and the one-third who had forgotten their kindness and questioned their love and intentions.

One might wonder why King Elohim didn't simply destroy Diablo and his followers at this point and erase them from existence. He certainly had the power to do it. But the deity king was much too wise to take the easiest course of action and blot out the disloyal subjects from life. For if he had, the loyal two-thirds would have always wondered if perhaps the king had done it only to silence an enemy who had actually been telling the truth about him.[9]

Of course, King Elohim could have also annihilated his betrayers and then removed even the memory of them from the minds of those who were left behind. This, he had the power to do also. But it wasn't the version of loyalty that he wanted, for it would have felt to him like their trust in him was built on deception. No, he and his son would have to take the most difficult path imaginable in order to truly make things right again. This, he was willing to do, but his heart ached whenever he thought about the things his beloved son would have to go through.

In an effort to take Prince Michael's mind off of his lost friendships and the difficult journey that lie ahead, King Elohim reminded him about the plans they'd been making before the war had interrupted them. They had dreamed of creating a new world together, and their brainstorming sessions had always brought his son so much happiness. It was this place that he wanted to bring the prince's heart back to. And so, the father and son set about to bring to life the designs their brilliant minds had previously only imagined.

For six evenings and six mornings, they did their work of creation meticulously, using a combination of the science, art, and humor that were within themselves. (Genesis 1:1-31) Inside this new world were breathtaking scenes of beauty. Skies of blue, pink, and orange filled with floating, white clouds. Sparkling aquamarine seas and waterfalls. Lush green lands with rolling hills, which grew fruit and vegetable-bearing trees and plants. Fragrant flowers of every color that never shriveled or faded. Eye-catching and plentiful gems made of countless types of unique stones and glass.

King Elohim and Prince Michael filled the skies, waters, and countryside with living creatures of all shapes and sizes. It was this part of their creative work that cheered the prince up most and caused him and his father to laugh until they cried. It felt so good for the king to see his son laugh again.

Outside of the new world's borders were magnificent luminous bodies that had been placed at just the right distances to provide the perfect amount of warmth and light for all of its inhabitants, day and night. One glowed, moved, and changed its shape cyclically, while the others twinkled and never left their posts. All of them were magnificent and faithfully shined light into the darkness at their appointed times.

On the sixth evening and morning, the deity father and son finished off their work of creation by making their crowning achievement—a being in their very own image. (Genesis 1:26-27) He looked like them physically, of course, but his likeness mirrored theirs in far more important ways. This perfect being—whom King Elohim and Prince Michael named Ansel—was endowed with their personality and moral nature, too. And the citizens of Bliss marveled at the fact that the deity father and son had craved the companionship of this new being enough to create him themselves, although they had always had each other and still had the praise of the loyal two-thirds.

On the evening and morning of the seventh day, King Elohim and his son rested from all of their work of creation.[10] As they beheld the world that they had made, they knew that it was good, and they could hardly contain their excitement as they thought about the exhilarating experience of the last six days. If only they could always feel this way. Happy. Carefree. *Worthy*. The deity father and son blessed the seventh day of each week and declared that it would henceforth become a perpetual day of rest for all living beings, in memorial and remembrance of this week of perfect creation.[11] (Genesis 2:1-3; Isaiah 66:23)

The man of their likeness was placed in an enchanted garden called Delight and visited regularly by the royal father and son. King Elohim and Prince Michael put all of the newly made creatures under the care of Ansel and allowed him to name them whatever he pleased. (Genesis 2:19-20) This occupied his heart and mind for some time—until he noticed something that he hadn't expected. Each of the many unique creatures had its own mate. "Where is mine?" he began to wonder. What the man didn't realize was that his creators knew him far better than he knew himself, and they had already designed his perfect match before he had even existed.

As if on cue, Ansel fell into a deep sleep. And with the enthusiasm that only the process of making a gift for a loved one can bring, the king and prince fashioned a soulmate for him from one of his own ribs. When he woke, Ansel was introduced to the lovely Emilyn by their creators. At first, he feared that his heart might burst. What was this feeling that had suddenly washed over him? He wanted to speak, but something was holding back his tongue. Knowing the unspoken thoughts of the man he had created, Prince Michael took the hand of Emilyn and placed it in Ansel's. (Genesis 2:21-25)

The first husband and wife loved each other deeply, and they loved King Elohim and Prince Michael even more for giving them the gift of marriage. Best friends and lovers, Ansel and Emilyn were inseparable as they lived happily—and innocently—in the Garden of Delight. Tending to the flowers, trees, and plants in their serene outdoor home never felt like work, only pleasure. Perfectly temperature-controlled with a tranquil breeze and the natural scents of Bliss, their home was everything they hadn't even known they'd wanted.

If the deity father and son could've protected Ansel and Emilyn from Diablo forever—while still ensuring their free will—they certainly would have. But these two things were inherently mutually exclusive. If the beings they created had been made without the ability to choose disobedience, then they would ultimately be little more than fancy robots. And their devotion would be meaningless. Even love itself is only the most treasured gift in the universe because it grows in minds that can just as easily decide *not* to love. One thought of a doll that was programmed by a toy maker to say, "I love you," over and over again with the pull of a string, is all it would take anyone who knew love's worth to be willing to take the risk of rejection and heartbreak. Neither did King Elohim want love and obedience that is solely dependent on the things he can provide. (Job 1:8-12)

No, there was never any question in the minds of King Elohim and Prince Michael that they would create the man and woman in their image with the ability to choose.[12] Not even the war and pain that had arisen from the free will they had given to the seraphim could ever make them feel differently. After all, the deity father and son had always known what Diablo and the one-third would choose. Like love, the principle of liberty was built into the very foundation of their kingdom and could not be changed—just as their commandments and character were immutable.

Unbeknownst to Ansel and Emilyn, evil existed just beyond their perfect garden home—and Diablo had already asked King Elohim for permission to approach them. Out of the necessity of fairness, his request had been granted.[13] For the king knew that love and loyalty *untested* are fragile. If there was no test, they could not choose to distrust him. How much then would their trust be worth?

Already, he had placed a tree in the middle of the Garden of Delight and named it the Tree of the Knowledge of Good and Evil. It was the only tree in the garden that the king had asked them not to eat from. (Genesis 2:17) And out of love, he had hoped to keep the knowledge of evil from them forever. They were free to eat from any other tree, particularly the Tree of Life, whose fruit kept them strong and healthy.

For a moment, even Diablo pondered what he was about to do. Did he really want to ruin the lives of the happy couple and condemn them to the unchangeable misery that he and the citizens who had followed him were now experiencing?[14] All too quickly, his self-serving resolve silenced the conscience that King Elohim had created within him, which was becoming weaker each time he ignored its promptings.

Diablo waited until Emilyn was alone to spin his web of lies because he knew that it would be far easier for him to sway one heart than two. And although the loyal seraphim had advised the pair not to separate—and even warned them about an enemy who might want to harm them[15]—Emilyn thought that she could trust her own instincts to keep herself safe. Once she had wandered out of Ansel's view and earshot, Diablo called her name. His voice was pleasant and soothing. Emilyn looked around but still couldn't tell where it was coming from. "Look up," Diablo instructed, and then she saw him—or at least the him he wanted her to see. (Genesis 3:1; 2 Corinthians 2:14)

Emilyn was enthralled with the unfamiliar being she saw before her within the branches of The Tree of Knowledge. A **talking** serpent? The royal deities had never shown her or Ansel anything like this before. *Why have they kept it from us?* she wondered silently. As if he had read her thoughts, the serpent offered up a plausible explanation to her inward question. "The King prefers that I stay in the background because He would rather keep my secret under wraps." "Secret?" an intrigued Emilyn reflexively asked. "You really don't know, do you?" Diablo said, to feign surprise and keep her guessing.

Diablo was too wise to tell pure lies and very intentionally wove truths into his speech of deception. He also knew that taking the form of a creature Emilyn had never seen before would give more credibility to his claims, which were centered on the possibility of attaining knowledge and powers that King Elohim wanted to keep for himself. "Did the king really tell you that you cannot eat from this particular tree?" the colorful serpent asked, pretending to inquire innocently. "King Elohim forbids it," Emilyn confirmed. "If we eat it—or even touch it—we will die." (Genesis 3:1-3)

Deliberately, Diablo touched the sparkling fruit and ate a bite himself nonchalantly. Emilyn was stunned. *Would the serpent now die?* she asked herself inwardly. Again, the unique creature appeared to have the power to read her mind. And he also knew her name. "No, Emilyn. I am not going to die. I've been eating from this tree for a while now, and it is the fruit of this particular tree that has made me so much wiser than I was before. In fact, it is this very fruit that gave me the power to speak.[16] King Elohim has only told you not to eat it because he knows that once you do, you will become as wise as he is." (Genesis 3:4-5)

Emilyn felt unsettled—and yet intrigued. This discovery made her question King Elohim's love and trustworthiness, and she didn't like that feeling. Pushing that disconcerting thought aside, she decided to focus on the exciting possibilities. For a moment, she considered asking the king about the serpent's claims, but just as quickly, she decided against it. If the talking serpent was telling the truth—and King Elohim was trying to keep her from becoming like him—then surely, he would simply reiterate his warning if she were to come to him with her questions.

In that instant, Emilyn decided to reach for the fruit before she lost her nerve. It tasted better than anything she had eaten before—at least that's what she convinced herself as she fantasized that she was also ascending to new heights intellectually.[17] In that same moment, Diablo experienced the euphoria that comes from winning an important victory—especially one that had never been guaranteed. Still unaware of what she had lost, Emilyn excitedly skipped through the garden to share her perceived enlightenment with her beloved husband. At first, the sight of his lover brought a smile to Ansel's face. There was a sparkle in her eyes that made her look even more beautiful and radiant than usual.

Just a moment later, as Ansel's eyes drifted downward, he saw it—the shimmery fruit in Emilyn's left hand. His face fell, and his heart sank simultaneously.[18] There was only one tree in the garden whose fruit had such an appearance—the Tree of the Knowledge of Good and Evil. Instinctively, he knew that his wife had been tricked by the enemy they had been warned about. Emilyn's fate was sealed. Of that much he was certain, although he understood that his wife did not yet recognize the tragedy that was already unfolding.

Ever aware of the inward thoughts of the beings they had created, King Elohim and Prince Michael listened keenly to the battle that Ansel was having with his conscience. "Trust *me*," the deity father and son whispered to his heart in unison, although they already knew what he was about to do. The heartache that Emilyn's choice had already brought them was about to be compounded by the decision of her husband, who couldn't imagine how it would be possible for them to preserve his happiness if he didn't follow his wife into sin.

Once Emilyn was done sharing Diablo's version of the truth with Ansel, her husband made it clear to her that he did not believe the serpent's claims. Terrified and frustrated that she had allowed herself to be deceived, he raised his voice and spoke unkindly to his wife for the very first time. His words cut deeply, but it wasn't only Emilyn's heart that felt unwell. Ansel didn't like this new tone of his voice either. Until now, they had never argued before. They didn't even know that it was possible to argue.

Determined to get along with his best friend once again—and ensure that they would not be separated—Ansel reached for the glistening piece of fruit from Emilyn's hand and quickly put it to his mouth. As he bit down into its sweet tasting center, he knew that it would cost him everything. But in that moment, he thought that it would be better to die with Emilyn than live without her.[19]

Neither of them could've possibly imagined what the Tree of the Knowledge of Good and Evil would teach them, or what it would mean to live in a world where Death—and Diablo—now reigned. They would learn that death from sin does not come instantly, but that the delay in their sentence would be as much of a burden as it was a blessing. Escorted from the garden home that they had loved so dearly and nurtured so effortlessly, they were now compelled to labor on land that did not yield its food without sweat and weariness. (Genesis 3:17-19) And although it would be nearly a millennium before Ansel and Emilyn would die themselves, it didn't take long for them to witness death.

First came the death of the animals that King Elohim used to make them clothing because they now understood that they were naked. (Genesis 3:21) Next came the withering of the flowers and plants that they had never seen while living in the Garden of Delight. Then came their worst nightmare—the death of their own child. Burying a child would have been horrific enough, but the tragedy was compounded by the fact that their firstborn son had caused the death of their other son with his own hands and uncontrolled jealousy and anger. (Genesis 4:8) And the citizens of Bliss marveled that the first murder to occur in the sinful world happened so quickly—in just the second generation.

But the first death didn't take the royal deity father and son by surprise. *This* was the evil they had wanted to keep Ansel and Emilyn from ever knowing about. Life and good things were the only knowledge their creators had hoped would be theirs. Yet, freedom of choice had topped the list of the gifts they had felt compelled to bestow on the pair, since they knew that without free will, true love cannot exist. If only Ansel and Emilyn's choices hadn't led them here.

The loyal citizens of Bliss had a front row seat to the show of horrors that naturally resulted from the sins of the human race—things that neither they nor the first parents could have ever foreseen or imagined. The degradation of their physical and mental powers would have been hard enough to watch, but the depths to which the human moral conscience sunk was especially difficult to witness and comprehend. Truly astonishing were the consequences of the freedoms that the seraphim once called Daystar had fought for, which proved to imprison all who sought them instead. And if King Elohim and Prince Michael had walked away and left the rebellious couple to suffer under the dictatorship of the self-serving and heartless leader they'd ultimately chosen, it would've been just. Mercifully, their story didn't end that way.

But saving the human family wouldn't come cheap. The sin that had infected their hearts and caused them to continually hurt each other could not be cured with mere words of forgiveness, nor could the sinners now trust and obey their creators in all circumstances simply because they wanted to. If only all of the riches of Bliss could have paid for and accomplished the sinners' healing. The love that King Elohim and Prince Michael had for the human family was great enough that they would have emptied the storehouses of all their treasures and paid any price, but the cure for sin could not be bought with gold or diamonds. Only the blood of the king's son himself could destroy the virus of sin that had damaged human hearts beyond all recognition. Only the death of Prince Michael could restore the trust of sinners in their king.[20]

So, the prince left his perfect kingdom—where he was so adored—and went on a 33-year-long mission to the dark world that imprisoned the lost and rebellious family he still loved. King Elohim could've asked his son not to go. He certainly wanted to—for his son was his greatest treasure. But the king himself loved the sin-sick human family. (John 3:16) It was a love that the loyal citizens of Bliss could not understand—and the **one** thing that made the family of Ansel and Emilyn so valuable.

What kind of deity prince would leave indescribable luxury and the worship of millions to be born in poverty and treated with such disdain? What kind of god would consent to Death to avenge the deaths of undeserving sinners? A hero of the greatest proportions. A hero who is worthy of unwavering trust and love. No other avenger is cooler. No other avenger can forgive and heal from sin.

And as Prince Michael hung on a cross to rescue his beloved sinners and free them from the chains that Diablo—and their own choices—had bound them with, the Kingdom of Bliss watched in awe. For four-thousand years, a tiny seed of doubt had lingered within the minds of the loyal seraphim.[21] Even as they had watched the misery of the human family and known that it had all began with the deceit of their fallen mentor, there had remained one question. Had he at least been right about the characters and motives of King Elohim and Prince Michael?

This day, all questions were answered. During these unspeakable moments, all doubts were finally erased. Their prince—and his own father—allowed things to happen to them that their accuser would never have consented to, let alone planned. The citizens of Bliss could not even begin to fully grasp the enormity of the sacrifice that the deity father and son had made to rescue *and heal* the wayward human family who had betrayed them. But what they did comprehend was more than enough to fully restore their trust in the creators Diablo had smeared.

It would be many more years before the intended recipients of the royal family's redemption would even begin to understand what the plan for their salvation had cost or why it was necessary. Along the way—although he knew that he had definitively lost the war at that cross—Diablo continued to do everything in his power to destroy the reputation of King Elohim and Prince Michael. He convinced others to attribute the results of sin and free will to their sinless creators—and when possible, he even attempted to hide their very existence. For those who would not accept these lies, he made up new ones. (John 8:44) Diablo created a counterfeit for every truth and commandment the royal family had ever designed—the things that were a part of their very natures and therefore could never be changed.[22]

In the end, Diablo's fiercest efforts could not overcome the power of the indestructible love that the fallen human family's creators had for them. Selflessness proved to be stronger than selfishness, and truth showed itself to be mightier than lies. Not every soul that the father and son sacrificed for would choose life. For many of them, the disease of sin appeared better than its hard-won cure. "For why will you die?" the one who died for them cried. (Ezek. 33:11 ESV) But he knew that he had to let them go, and he gave them up to the sins they desired. (Psalms 81:12) Of the numbers saved, there could've been more—there *should've* been more. Yet, Prince Michael would never regret his suffering. For *just one* soul, he would've done the same.[23] (Matthew 18:12)

******

And *this* is the definition of the ultimate hero. This was the much-abbreviated story of the **Absolute Avenger**. Our greatest Hollywood champions would never defend the bad guy. Our most admirable real-life rescuers would never die for the ones they knew would murder them. Yet, that is exactly what Jesus Christ, the Son of God and Creator of the Universe, did for us—and so much more. If you already love Him, then tell Him every day, and share this story with someone who has never heard it. And if you don't love Him—or aren't even convinced that He actually exists—then first open your heart to the possibility, and ask someone you trust for help. Search for Him as you would for buried treasure, because your life depends on it, and *you will find Him*.

EPILOGUE

This book had already been written. It was finished, and all of the words in my heart had been said. But the King of the Multiverse wasn't done speaking. He wasn't through with the story that I'm supposed to share—and *you* were meant to read. This final tale is just another real-life example of our Heavenly Father's providence—the providence that my children and I never even knew we needed until it had already been provided.

The groundwork for God's plan of protection had been laid many years before. I didn't recognize it at the time, of course, and simply viewed it through the lens of my mother's historically overprotective nature. "Don't sit too close to the steering wheel," she had cautioned me more than once as a teenager. "If you're too close to the steering wheel during a crash, the force of the airbag can kill you." That wasn't the end of her warning either, for she wasn't about to leave my interpretation of her instructions to chance. "Your arms should be nearly straight when you're driving," my mother explained. "And your knees shouldn't be bent that much," she continued, as she pointed to their nearly ninety-degree angle (which had seemed perfectly suitable to my sixteen-year-old self at the time).

The advice my mother gave me had initially left me sitting so far from the steering wheel that it felt like I was a little girl whose legs couldn't possibly be expected to reach the gas pedal. *That* seemed to be an obvious danger of its own, of course. (So, I would be lying if I said that the driver's seat of the 1995 Honda Accord never moved from the position that my mother had deemed safe.) Still, her point had been made, and its effect was long-lasting.

Decades passed. And as is typical of parenthood, the time of my own daughters' driving debuts snuck up on me and came long before I was ready. With amusement, I watched both girls sit much closer to the steering wheel than I ever had. Their eerily similar positions appeared uncomfortable, unsafe, and even comical. Sometimes, I pointed it out and asked them to move the seat back, while other times, I simply said nothing—or at least nothing motherly and protective—because it seemed easier to tease them into pushing their seat away from the steering wheel than to explain the gory details about what could happen if they didn't.

These details my own mother had made sure to share with teenage me, of course: a broken neck, serious injury to the heart or head, and even instant death—all of which are more likely to happen to drivers below a certain height and weight, such as my two girls. I held this list of unpleasant possibilities deep within the recesses of my brain, the place where our remote memories go to hibernate and wait for their chance to be thought of once again someday. And while this memory waited patiently for its turn, I forgot all about it. Had it not been for Providence, it probably would have been forgotten still. But Heaven had other plans, as it often d oes.

There was no other reason that I should think to warn my girls about the dangers of sitting too close to the steering wheel again on that particular Sabbath afternoon. Sure, I knew that it would be the last time I would see my oldest daughter for a while, since Meliah was about to start her freshman year of college in just two days. But she didn't have a car yet—or even have her driver's license—so why did I suddenly feel the need to tell her about the risks of an ill-positioned airbag deployment as we were leaving to go to lunch at her Great Aunt Joan's house? Stranger still was the fact that although I had already moved on to another topic by the time her younger sister Makenzie got in the van, I somehow felt compelled to stop this new conversation dead in its tracks so that I wouldn't forget to warn her, too. And having relayed the advice that had suddenly come to mind a second time, she nodded in acknowledgment the way that children do, when you're not certain that your parental advice will actually be taken to h eart.

A couple of days later, it was time to say goodbye to Meliah and make the nine-hour road trip home to Maryland in Tan Van (the name that a Chick-fil-A employee had once given our 2008 Toyota Sienna van, which eventually stuck as we began to develop a love-hate relationship with "him" after thirteen years). Makenzie had driven most of the way to Michigan, just four days earlier, and had proven herself to be a responsible chauffeur, who wasn't easily distracted. So, as we started the long journey back, with Makenzie at the wheel and Ryder sitting directly behind her, there was no reason to think that our return trip wouldn't be just as smooth as our drive to Michigan had been. Still, we prayed. The three of us prayed for traveling mercies like we always do when we pull out of the driveway at the start of a long car ride. We asked our Heavenly Father to keep us safe, and then we thought of it no more—but *He* did. God remembered every word.

Three hours into our journey, it began to rain quite heavily. I asked Makenzie if she wanted me to trade places with her, but she felt comfortable enough with the road conditions to keep driving. An hour later, the rain lightened up, and our visibility was much better. I was relieved that the worst of the weather seemed to be behind us, and we continued on.

Halfway through our nine-hour drive, we entered a two-lane construction zone on the Ohio Turnpike. There was little-to-no shoulder on the driver's side of the left lane, so the cars in that lane felt compelled to move closer to us in the right lane—but I didn't notice. And what I *was* aware of—the miles-long, three-inch drop-off that lie on my side of the right lane—Makenzie's 5 foot 2 inch frame couldn't see. Faithfully, she steered clear of the orange and white warning barrels on the passenger's side of the right lane that she was able to see. If only they hadn't been spaced so far apart....

Suddenly, I saw it—Tan Van's front passenger side wheel careening toward the sharp drop-off of our wet interstate road and my child blissfully oblivious to the danger that lie just seconds away. Instinctively, I screamed out the best warning I could muster, knowing that even a three-inch drop would likely cause us to hydroplane in the rain—especially if my daughter wasn't expecting it. Still unaware of the specific peril that awaited her on the right side of the road—but now at least conscious of the fact that she didn't want to be near it—we both hoped silently that there would be enough time to avoid the crash that we had already begun to fear.

Chance couldn't afford to grant us our wish, however, for it was simply too late. Our last remaining seconds had been spent, and nothing that happened after they were gone would be in our control. As Tan Van's passenger side wheels slipped over the edge of the narrowed right lane, Makenzie jerked the steering wheel leftward, overcorrecting unintentionally and causing him to spin out of control.

In the seconds that followed, there was no time to call out to God as I had always assumed that there would be in such a crisis. More than once in the months leading up to this terrifying day, I had dreamt that I was driving alone on a dark highway, when suddenly my car lights stopped working, and I could no longer see the road in front of me. As the pitch-black night obscures my view in this dream, I have no idea where I am going—and strangely, there is no option to put my foot on the break and simply stop driving. My vehicle continues to take me into an unknown abyss. I can sense that I am falling over a cliff—and at that moment, I cover my head with both arms and cry out to God for help. Perhaps even those desperate pleas from my recurring dream were honored by the Creator of the Multiverse in the moment that came later, when I was unable to voice them even silently.

Our real-life calamity caused Makenzie and I to close our eyes and cover our heads with our hands reflexively, just as I had done in my dreams. Never in my forty-five years had any of the previous car accidents I experienced caused me to do this. With each of the other wrecks, my eyes had remained open. And never before had I been unable to even imagine where my car would end up after the dreaded impending impact.

How different and horrifying this accident was! No seconds remained to anticipate the very real possibility of death—or mentally prepare for it. Had our lives been lost that day, we wouldn't have known it was coming. As Tan Van changed his course by ninety degrees and headed for the cement barrier or Jersey Wall on the other side of the left lane, we simply gave up and accepted our fate....

It was the power of the collision that woke Makenzie and I from our frozen state. Never before had we experienced a force of this magnitude or a sound so terrible. With Tan Van now stopped dead in his tracks and our eyes reopened, Makenzie and I could see that our airbags had deployed, though we had no memory of it. Still in shock, it took us a few more seconds to comprehend that we had survived—and once we did, there was no time to be grateful, for our thoughts immediately turned to each other. W as *everyone* alive?

For better or worse, I knew that I had to find out. First, I saw Makenzie's face, and the obvious signs of life within her eyes filled my entire body with relief. "Is everyone okay?" I asked, with competing emotions of fear and hope, as I dared to look in the back seat at my youngest baby. What I discovered looking back at me gave me a feeling that I can only describe as the exact opposite of those moments in our lives when our heart sinks with unexpected and utter disappointment. Although not free of *all* traces of the ride of terror that we had just taken together, Ryder's expression also contained hints of bravery and innocence. I was thankful that he had been spared a front row seat during Tan Van's sudden metamorphosis into a roller coaster.

Seconds later, there was a knock on my passenger side window. Two men were standing there, so I opened the window. "Is everybody alright?" the man in the front inquired. The look of concern on their faces was obviously genuine. "I think we're okay," I muttered softly, as some feelings of embarrassment began to creep in.

I was the adult who had ultimately allowed this accident to happen, after all. The should haves, would haves, and could haves swirled around inside my head, until they became the perfect ingredients to bake a cake of guilt, which suddenly felt like a heavy rock within my gut. If only I had warned Makenzie about the drop-off *miles earlier*, instead of assuming that she could see it. Better yet, why hadn't I simply told her that I preferred to drive until we were out of the construction zone?

A question from our Good Samaritan strangers brought my attention back to the present. "Can you put the gear in neutral?" I looked at the gear selector below the instrument panel and saw that it was already in neutral, though Makenzie obviously hadn't shifted the gear out of drive herself. As we both examined the gear shift more closely and noticed that it was stuck in its new position, we were grateful that it was at least in the position it needed to be.

It was then that I saw it—Makenzie's knees and the dashboard. Not a single inch of space separated them. I didn't yet understand the significance of what I was seeing. But even in that moment, I recognized that my child's legs had nearly been crushed in the impact. My eyes remained fixed on this sobering discovery until I began to feel Tan Van moving backwards.

Our Good Samaritans pushed him away from the Jersey Wall with such ease that it felt like Tan Van's massive luggage-laden, two-ton body was simply being driven in reverse. The engineless ride to the construction zone through two lanes of halted interstate traffic was swift. On the other side was the ambulance that had been waiting for us. "They'll take care of you now," the two strangers said next before asking, "Is there anything else that you need?" "I don't think so," I answered, hoping it was really true. Makenzie would later tell us that she watched them as they walked away and saw them high five each other—one calling the other by name and saying, "Good job"—before they got into two separate cars and drove off.

The paramedic gave us his attention next and asked me for permission to examine each child inside the ambulance. When he was finished, he told me that given the severity of the accident, further evaluation in the emergency room was recommended—but I could sign a waiver should I decide to decline this transport to the hospital on my children's behalf. There was a reason for his caution, and he didn't need to say it out loud, for I already knew what he was thinking. What if there is a slow internal bleed that will simply take longer to manifest itself?

I signed the waivers for both Makenzie and Ryder and wondered if I was making a mistake. My right knee felt bruised, but I couldn't see any discoloration. There were no visible injuries on any of us. Still, I limped a bit as I walked short distances in the perilous construction zone, my arms filled with the seemingly important "stuff" that Tan Van would no longer be able to carry for us.

By all appearances, Tan Van had clearly fared less well in the crash than his familiar occupants. His face was hardly recognizable, having folded inward like an accordion—but obviously not as neatly. One of his hubcaps was missing. My eyes scanned the construction zone first, and then the interstate, until I saw it lying across both lanes of traffic by the Jersey Wall (now marred by ugly black imprints from the unintended impact that I already wanted to forget).

Cars whizzed by—too many to count—and I wondered how the steady flow of afternoon commuters had strangely stopped as my children's side of Tan Van lie perpendicular and fully exposed to the oncoming traffic. In their most vulnerable moment, something inexplicable had happened. How was it possible that not a single car had hit them? My thoughts were interrupted by the paramedic's goodbye.

After the ambulance left, it was the young state trooper's turn to question us next. He had only just arrived because he'd been called to the scene of another accident a few miles away before ours. Makenzie's face couldn't hide the guilt and disappointment that she was feeling inside, and Trooper K. recognized that he had an opportunity to help her with her most pressing need. It wasn't the mandatory citation for failing to control her vehicle that would teach Makenzie the biggest lesson of the day—although he was still required to give it to her because she was a minor, and the state of Ohio mandated it in such cases.

Instead, it was the confession of the intimidating authority figure himself that helped my sixteen-year-old daughter to start down the path toward self-forgiveness. "I caused two accidents of my own before I even turned 18," Trooper K. revealed to Makenzie. For just a moment, she allowed herself to relax—and even make it halfway to a smile. But then the gloom returned.

Still in shock, as I was, Makenzie's teenage heart also had to contend with the competing emotions of shame and defeat as she thought about the prospect of having to start her nine-month period of monitored driving all over again (according to the state of Maryland's rules for those with a learner's permit who get a speeding ticket or cause an accident). Only an hour before, she had been planning to take her driver's test the very next week. The long-awaited appointment had already been scheduled, and Makenzie had anticipated that she would walk out of the DMV with a driver's license in her hand. But now her dream seemed out of reach.

Trooper K. made plans with the tow truck driver to meet us at a hotel a couple of exits away. The personification of Tan Van intensified as we emptied him of all of our belongings and knew instinctively that we would never see our loyal friend again. After everything of value had been transferred to the tow truck, Trooper K. took us to the first hotel we came to, and I went inside to ask for a room. The woman at the front desk told me that there were no available rooms, and I wondered for a moment if it was my appearance that had prompted her response. Much of the right side of my favorite purple Ron Jon Surf Shop T-shirt was now coated with an unfamiliar substance from the airbag deployment and also felt stiff, as if it had been stained by white paint and then starched five times over. I probably looked as disheveled as I felt inside. "Okay," I muttered—because I didn't have the strength to say anything else.

As I stood there in unexpected defeat, Trooper K. walked in to verify that I'd checked in. When I told him that there were no rooms, he turned and looked at the hotel employee with an expression that clearly said, "Seriously?" Now it was her turn to be surprised. Clearly, she hadn't expected me to have an advocate in the form of a police officer, and this advocate of mine asked her to do what she hadn't offered to do before—call the hotel next door to ask if *they* had a room. "We don't have phone numbers for the other hotels," she responded matter-of-factly. But young Trooper K. wasn't satisfied with her excuse and let her know with his face that he would not be taking no for an answer. "I guess I could look them up on my phone," she finally offered.

A few minutes later, we arrived at the hotel next door, which the previous hotel's desk clerk had verified was still accepting new guests. The kids and I went in to start the check-in process, and the woman at this desk quoted me a price of $130 for the night. I nodded and handed her my credit card. A moment later, Trooper K. came into the hotel lobby and walked right up to a somber Makenzie. "It's going to be okay," he attempted to reassure her, before reminding her that he had *twice* been in her shoes as a teenager. After observing their interaction, the hotel clerk announced that she would be charging me a discounted rate of $80 for our room.

I thanked her, of course, and then watched the tow truck driver bring in the fully-loaded Bellman's cart that he had filled to the brim with our luggage and belongings—the many things that the ever-faithful Tan Van would now be unable to carry the rest of the way to Maryland for us. As we said our goodbyes to Trooper K. and the tow truck driver, I took one last look at Tan Van through the hotel lobby's glass doors and knew that I would never see him again. With keycards in hand, the kids and I walked to the elevator in silence and struggled to maneuver the heavy-laden Bellman's cart on the way to our room.

A sense of relief began to intermingle with the shock and regret. I thought that I should've done more to prevent the crash, yet I was grateful that we were all alive. Still frozen emotionally, I collapsed in the chair that I found in the corner of our room and listened passively to the phone conversation that Makenzie was having with her father. I didn't feel like talking to anyone myself, and this spirit of silence only grew stronger when it became clear that my ever-practical husband was surprised and frustrated that I hadn't called our auto insurance company yet.

Now *I* was the one who felt frustrated. How could Jason be focused on an insurance claim so soon after an accident that had nearly taken our lives? Where was the man who usually brought the comfort? The more he insisted that I needed to call our car insurance company *right away*, the more upset I became. And before long, we found ourselves in the middle of an argument.

As my emotions spilled out, it seemed easier to raise my voice than to cry—because I definitely did *not* want to cry. "You have no idea what we went through today!" I shot back to Jason in response. "You're acting like this is one of the typical car accidents that we've experienced before, just because we all survived. It was *nothing* like any of those other crashes. We actually thought that we might die!" It was all I could say, so I said no more, but I had already said too much in my daughter's presence.

Makenzie's eyes filled with tears, and then she walked out of our hotel room. Instantly, I felt even worse. Why couldn't I have spared her this additional heartache of listening to her parents fight and discovering how traumatic it had been for her mother? She was already feeling guilty enough, and my instincts told me that she was going to blame herself for these things now, too. I knew that I had to find Makenzie and make things right, but I was worried about leaving nine-year-old Ryder alone in the hotel room. So, I put off my search—hoping that she would come back on her own—and, as I waited a little longer, I made the unwanted phone call to the Erie Insurance company.

With the dreaded task of relaying our guilt-laden trauma now behind me, I began to feel unsettled about my missing daughter. *I can't think about anything else until I find Makenzie*, my heart told my brain. And that was that. I set out on my mission. First, I showed Ryder how to chain and deadbolt the hotel room door behind me. "Don't answer it for anyone but me or your sister," I instructed him (and then made him promise, for good measure). Then I did what any modern-day mother would do in search of her lost child. I enlisted the help of the Find My iPhone app. (And I was grateful for it!)

Aimlessly, I wandered around the hotel, until I saw that the small blue dot representing my location in the app was actually moving farther away from the miniature picture of my girl. After I changed course and headed in the opposite direction, the distance between the blue dot and Makenzie's tiny photo began to decrease. But strangely, as I continued to walk, the space increased once again. Frustrated, I stopped moving so that I could analyze the locations on the app more carefully. It was then that I saw it—a steep flight of stairs positioned directly across from me on the other side of the hotel's parking lot. I had no idea where they would lead me but decided to climb them anyways, and as I did, the app made it clear that I was getting closer to Makenzie.

Finally, I saw my child when there were no more stairs to climb. There she sat on the pavement, in an entirely new parking lot that lie hidden behind shrubbery, high above the one below it. For a moment, I hesitated to intrude upon the quiet place that Makenzie had clearly gone to escape. Wasn't it enough to calm my mother's heart that I had found her safe and sound? With these things in mind, I sat down at the top of the stairs and quietly waited while my daughter talked softly to an unknown voice on the other end of her cell phone.

Eventually, Makenzie's eyes met mine, but their usual light was missing. In its place, I saw something else. Was it fear? And if it was, had this fear been born from the day's trauma? Or was my child afraid of what I might say next instead? I didn't want either possibility to be true.

There was only one thing to say, and I knew it. I *felt* it, too. "I'm sorry," I told Makenzie, as I watched her face closely for any signs of forgiveness. I couldn't wait for them, however, before the rest of my apology came spilling out. "I should never have argued with Dad in front of you—or said that this was the most traumatic thing that I'd ever experienced. I was just frustrated that he was acting like it was a typical accident and didn't seem to understand what we went through. But I realize now that hearing me talk about how traumatic the accident was for me wasn't something that you needed to hear, because you've already been feeling bad enough. I want to stress again that this wasn't your fault, Honey."

As my child absorbed my explanation, I could see her begin to relax. And when she did, she was finally able to share the story that would forever change the way I view that seemingly good-for-nothing day. I could never have imagined the Providence that had clearly altered the outcome of our accident for my precious Makenzie—or the lengths that our Heavenly Father had gone to ensure her safety, beginning *decades* earlier with the seeds He planted through my mother. It isn't often that we are given the opportunity to peek behind the curtain and see the hand of God move on our behalf so plainly, but this would prove to be one of those times. Of course, His involvement in the circumstances of our lives isn't infrequent—but the gift of our awareness of it on this side of Heaven usually is.

Only in hindsight could Makenzie understand that the voice in her head that she'd thought was her own had really been the still small voice of the Holy Spirit. Why would she have thought otherwise, after all? Now *you* be the judge, as I relay my daughter's memories of this once-in-a-lifetime day.

The day had started with a "safe trip prayer," as my parents had called our custom when they taught me to pray it. Around the time of this prayer—with my previous warning in mind—Makenzie had moved her seat away from the steering wheel very intentionally, just as we started the nine-hour ride home. Hours passed. Our journey had been uneventful so far, and there was no reason to believe that it wouldn't end this way, too. But the Future Teller knew otherwise.

Thirty minutes before impact, a voice inside my daughter's head told her that she was still too close to the steering wheel. *Move the seat back a little more*, she heard distinctly. And in response to the idea that she assumed had come from her own thoughts, she reached for the seat position adjustment control on the lower left side of the driver's seat and pulled the electronic lever backwards until her seat was a few inches farther from the steering wheel. Still unaware of the impending danger, my sixteen-year-old drove on, as she and Ryder listened happily to the music from her iPhone's playlist through Tan Van's speakers.

Five minutes before impact, the inner voice spoke again. But this time, the voice that my daughter still presumed to be her own called her by name—and used a unit of measurement that she normally doesn't. *Kenzie, just three centimeters more*. Immediately, she followed the advice of her inner dialogue and somehow knew that the words in her brain were referring to a safer distance between her seat and the steering wheel. Only later in hindsight would she consider the fact that talking to herself in the third person isn't her thing—or that she's an inches girl from the United States and would never think in units from the metric system.

Even at this point, I knew with certainty that this unexpected revelation by Makenzie had my Abba's name written all over it. It would be hours before either of us would understand the precision with which the Holy Spirit's instruction had been given, however. And our minds and bodies were still silently preoccupied with the unprecedented force of the crash we had survived.

The sun was beginning to set, and our clocks told us that it was time for supper, so Makenzie and I picked up Ryder from the hotel room, though neither of us actually felt hungry. All three of us crossed four busy lanes of traffic on foot—two heading in each direction, with a median in between—because the restaurants were on the opposite side of the street. I limped along the way but didn't know why, because my right leg didn't appear to be visibly injured. Very intentionally, I said nothing about the pain, for it seemed to me that any mention of it would do no good and might even make Makenzie feel worse instead.

Ryder ate our makeshift supper of Sonic fries and shakes happily at first, but he asked to cut it short when he noticed that sundown had arrived. "I don't want to go back on that road when it's dark. What if the cars can't see us?" he asked, with a worried expression on his face. "It'll be okay," I tried to reassure him, but he wasn't convinced. Again, Ryder voiced his concerns about the prospect of running back to the hotel while dodging cars that might not see us in the dark. I knew that I could get us safely back to our hotel, regardless of the time of day, but it felt more important to take this particular burden off of my nine-year-old's heart than to play the "trust me" card. After all, he had already experienced something bad on a road this very day that hadn't been likely to happen.

Once we were back inside our hotel, the three of us tried to act like we were simply on a planned vacation, in spite of the fact that our room was strewn with the countless, random contents of Tan Van that had taken years to accumulate. Normally, our family likes to watch television in the evenings when we stay in a hotel together. But this time, no one fought over the channel or even looked at the screen, so we decided to go to bed early. As we put our pajamas on, we noticed our bruises for the first time. Although it had taken hours for them to appear, there were many.

From youngest to oldest, we surveyed the damage together. On Ryder, there was a hematoma—or deeper collection of blood—over the right side of his abdomen, in the area of his liver. Bruises also colored the imprint that his seatbelt had made on the left side of his neck during the crash. But for Makenzie, the marks of Tan Van's collision with the cement barrier wall were even wider spread. Blue and purple reminders of the impact covered much of her chest and *both* sides of her neck. Then, there was my right knee. Finally, I could see the external evidence of the injury that I'd already been feeling, as the joint swelling was now obvious, and a trail of bruises marched down my leg on the inside of my calf.

When there were no more external injuries to discover, it only seemed fitting to say thank you to the One who had protected us from so much worse. The three of us knelt down in the middle of our hotel room and took turns praying to the God of the Universe, who had not only *seen* us, but had seen us when we didn't even know that we needed Him. It's difficult to describe the feeling that this realization filled my own heart with, but if I must choose a word, I will settle for this one: awe. Already, I felt awe—though there was more to discover.

With the lights out and our room quiet, I fully intended to fall asleep as quickly as I normally do. Instead, I simply lay there while my brain worked out at the gym. I'll never know how long my mind would've resisted the rest my body craved because a soft cry from the next bed interrupted my thoughts. Even if the room had been filled with a hundred nine-year-old boys, no time would've been needed to determine whose whimper it was, for a mother knows the cry of her child. What I couldn't have known, however, was that the reason for my son's cry was an all-too-familiar fear that I didn't realize he was capable of imagining.

Almost in unison, Makenzie and I—his two protectors—called out into the dark room and asked the same question, "What's wrong, Ryder?" Without hesitation, he revealed the source of his anxiety. "I'm afraid to go to sleep. What if there's something wrong with my heart, and I don't wake up?" I was stunned, but not for the reasons you might think. As I thought about how to respond, Makenzie surprised me further by echoing her brother's sentiments. "I'm afraid to go to sleep, too! What if I have a brain bleed?"

What neither of them knew—because I had barely admitted it to myself at this point—was that I had already considered the possibility that I might not wake up in the morning. Even worse, I had actually pictured a morbid scene, in which the kids find me dead in the hotel bed the next day. The cause of my demise? A slow but steady bleed in my brain, chest, or abdomen—too small to cause pain or make me feel lightheaded, so it remained undetected, silently robbing me of my blood during the night, until it was too late to save me. Never before in the hours following a car accident had I thought about such things, but *this* one? The force of this collision was indescribable.

In forty-five years, my body hadn't known a force of this magnitude. And it had seemed to me that it was my physician's brain that couldn't help but dream up the worst case scenarios. Yet, it was now apparent that both of my children—having no medical knowledge at all—had still instinctively feared the same morbid medical outcomes. It could only mean one thing: My mind hadn't exaggerated the force of the collision's impact. The assumption that it had been powerful enough to cause internal bleeding was evidently universal. Our sample size may have only been three, but we were the only three who would ever know what that moment had felt like.

At this point, there was only one thing to do. Pray again. But first, I let Makenzie and Ryder know that they were not alone in their anxiety and particular concern. The discovery of our shared fear proved to be therapeutic in and of itself, of course. Yet only a conversation with God could truly calm our uneasiness and give us the real peace that we needed. "Since we're still scared, it sounds like we need to pray again," I told the kids.

And so, we got back up and met at the foot of our beds. Again, we knelt down together (on five out of our six knees) and took turns praying to the One who had already saved us. We told our Heavenly Father about the specific fear that we had *all* been keeping inside, and then we laid it at His feet. "Help me to wake up in the morning," the youngest and most innocent of us asked God plainly, when it was finally his turn. Last but not least were the words of a child when the ears of Heaven listened intently that night. And far lighter the three of us felt upon standing than we had felt before bowing to the omnipotent and tenderhearted King.

These things I pondered in my heart as I got back into bed. No longer weighed down by worry, I turned on my iPad, rather than immediately closing my eyes and attempting to fall asleep. Normally, I scroll through social media at bedtime, but this time, I found myself looking at the day's photos instead. One picture, in particular, caught my attention—the one that Makenzie had (fairly) questioned the need for in the first place, when I had taken it moments after the crash.

There she was, sitting in front of Tan Van's steering wheel following the airbag deployment. Since it was only after exiting the vehicle that we had been able to visualize the dashboard's new position—much closer to Makenzie—and I hadn't yet known about her decision to move her seat backwards three different times before impact, I couldn't possibly have understood the significance of her body's position in this photo at the time it was taken. But now? It told an incredible story that was hard to miss.

From the photo, with its side view of Makenzie, it was easy to see that there was less than an inch of space remaining between her knees and the dashboard. The words she had shared with me flashed back to my mind. It wasn't enough that she had thought to push her seat back farther at the start of our road trip, as we prayed for safety. Twice more she had been impressed to move it back even farther—to the place where it would stop forever and find *no room to spare*. "**Kenzie, just three centimeters more,**" the voice inside her head had said, only five minutes before impact. And though my daughter doesn't think in centimeters, her physician mom often does.

As I stared at the picture of my child's knees and Tan Van's dashboard, there was no need to wonder how many centimeters of space lie between them—for I had memorized the conversion factor for centimeters and inches long ago. One inch equals 2.54 centimeters. So, I knew intuitively that three centimeters must equal just over one inch.... The precision with which Heaven had protected her made my heart feel things it rarely gets to experience in this life—things that I could never fully describe. In that moment, I knew with certainty that God had preserved Makenzie's legs, but naturally I wondered if there was more to Heaven's behind-the-scene efforts. Had He also saved her life?

Over the next few days—after Jason's parents had come to our rescue and taken us the rest of the way home—the unseen bruises darkened and made themselves known. From knee to ankle, they colored my now-swollen right leg and made it painful to walk or even rest. Over young Ryder's liver region was an unintended painting of purple, blue, and yellow hues. And Makenzie? On the girl who had heard and heeded the whispers of the Spirit of God Himself were numerous violet marks on her chest and neck. I stared at the bruises on my sixteen-year-old from the airbag and tried to analyze their pattern.

Why exactly had my own mother tried to warn me about sitting too close to the steering wheel as she did? Airbags save lives, after all—as long as we don't put our children under the age of twelve in the front seat, right? Seconds later, my mother's words echoed within my brain once again, and I found myself roaming the internet in search of the answers I craved. It didn't take long to find them.

ENDNOTES

Prologue

1. Ellen G. White, *The Great Controversy* (Nampa, ID: Pacific Press Publishing Association, 2002).

Abba Knows Best

1. Paul Aurandt, *Paul Harvey's The Rest of the Story* (New York: Bantam Books, 1984).

Brilliant with Dementia

1. Water Within, "The Backwards Kingdom," track 4 on *The Backwards Kingdom*, Independent, 2019, compact disc.

2. Jamie Ducharme, "Stephen Hawking Was an Atheist. Here's What He Said About God, Heaven and His Own Death," *Time*, March 14, 2018, https://time.com/5199149/stephen-hawking-death-god-atheist/.

Faithful Even When We Won't Remember

1. Lyrics.com, STANDS4 LLC, 2022. **"God Will Make a Way Lyrics."** Accessed June 13, 2022. https://www.lyrics.com/lyric/5212552/Don+Moen/God+Will+Make+a+Way .

2. Ellen G. White, *Steps to Christ* (Battle Creek, MI: Review and Harold, 1898), 99-100.

Hot Pepper Sisters

1. Diana Nollen, "Cedar Rapids Sisters Say 'We Do' to 'Don't' Game Show, Showing Thursday," *The Gazette*, July 8, 2020, https://www.thegazette.com/art/cedar-rapids-sisters-say-we-do-to-dont-game-show-showing-thursday/.

I Can Fix It

1. DIY Auto Repair Videos, "Removing Scratches from Your Car Using WD-40 Hack - Final Judgement," August 29, 2015, educational video, 4:36, https://www.youtube.com/watch?v=oKLXVNHbcvw.

Stick With Him

1. Walter E. Rollins, "Frosty the Snowman Lyrics," Lyrics.com, Accessed May 21, 2022.

2. Graham Maxwell, *Can God Be Trusted?* (Redlands, CA: Pine Knoll Publications, 2002), 43.

3. Maxwell, *Can God Be Trusted?* 43.

4. Water Within, "The Backwards Kingdom," 2019.

A Tale of Two Hearts

1. White, *The Great Controversy*, 492-504.

Restoration

1. *Hand Built Hot Rods*. Directed by Tim Vincent. Aired 2018-present, on MotorTrend.

2. *Hot Rod TV*. "Pure Vision." Directed by Dennis Zerull. Episode aired Feb 28, 2009, on MotorTrend.

3. Calvary Worship, "You Restore," Lyrics.com, Accessed September 29, 2024.

Transmission

1. Andrew Robinson, "Did Einstein Really Say That?" *Nature*, April 30, 2018, https://www.nature.com/articles/d41586-018-05004-4.

It'll Be Okay in the End

1. "Toddlers & Tiaras," IMDb, accessed June 16, 2022, https://www.imdb.com/title/tt1364951/?ref_=ttfc_fc_tt.

2. "Wanda Holloway Trial: 1991," Encyclopedia.com, accessed June 16, 2022, https://www.encyclopedia.com/law/law-magazines/wanda-holloway-trial-1991.

The Unrequited Hug

1. Francis Bacon, *The Essayes or Counsels, Civill and Morall, of Francis Lo. Verulam, Viscount St. Alban.* (1625), *Of Boldnesse*.

The Tattered Kingdom

1. Lee Greenwood, "God Bless the USA," recorded 1984, track B5 on *You've Got a Good Love Comin'*, Panorama Records, 1984, LP.

The Job Moments

1. Toni Weschler, *Taking Charge of Your Fertility: The Definitive Guide to Natural Birth Control and Pregnancy Achievement* (New York City: Harper Perennial Paperback, 1995).

2. History.com Editors, "Teen gunman kills 17, injures 17 at Parkland, Florida high school," *History*, February 6, 2019, https://www.chica gomanualofstyle.org/tools_citationguide/citation-guide-1.html.

The Absolute Avenger

1. *Spider-Man: No Way Home*, directed by Jon Watts (Columbia Pictures and Marvel Studios, 2021), 148 minutes.

2. *Avengers: Infinity War*, directed by Russo, Joe, and Anthony Russo (United States: Walt Disney Studios Motion Pictures, 2018), 149 minutes.

3. *Avengers: Endgame*, directed by Russo, Anthony, and Joe Russo (United States: Walt Disney Studios Motion Pictures, 2019), 182 minutes.

4. Ellen G. White, *Patriarchs and Prophets* (Washington D.C.: Review and Harold Publishing Association, 1890), 34.

5. Maxwell, *Can God Be Trusted?* 14.

6. White, *Patriarchs and Prophets*, 36.

7. White, *Patriarchs and Prophets*, 37.

8. White, *Patriarchs and Prophets*, 38-40.

9. White, *Patriarchs and Prophets*, 42.

10. Maxwell, *Can God Be Trusted?* 128-129.

11. White, *Patriarchs and Prophets*, 47-48.

12. Ellen G. White, *The Story of Redemption* (Hagerstown, MD: Review and Herald Publishing Association, 1947), 28-31.

13. White, *Patriarchs and Prophets*, 50-53.

14. White, *The Story of Redemption*, 28-31

15. White, *The Story of Redemption*, 28-31

16. White, *Patriarchs and Prophets*, 54.

17. White, *The Story of Redemption*, 35.

18. White, *The Story of Redemption*, 28-31

19. White, *Patriarchs and Prophets*, 56

20. Maxwell, *Can God Be Trusted?* 71-83.

21. Ellen G. White, "It Is Finished," in *The Desire of Ages*, ed. Marion Davis (Mountain View, Calif, Portland, Or: Pacific Press Pub. Association, 1940), 758-764.

22. White, *The Great Controversy*, 433.

23. Ellen G. White, *Christ's Object Lessons* (Washington D.C.: Review and Herald Publishing Association, 1900), 187.

BIBLIOGRAPHY

1. White, Ellen G. *The Great Controversy*. Nampa, ID: Pacific Press Publishing Association, 2002.

2. Aurandt, Paul. *Paul Harvey's The Rest of the Story*. New York: Bantam Books, 1984.

3. Water Within. "The Backwards Kingdom." Recorded September 2019. Track 4 on *The Backwards Kingdom*. Independent, 2019, compact disc.

4. Ducharme, Jamie. "Stephen Hawking Was an Atheist. Here's What He Said About God, Heaven and His Own Death." *Time*, March 14, 2018. https://time.com/5199149/stephen-hawking -death-god-atheist/.

5. Moen, Don. "God Will Make a Way Lyrics." Lyrics.com. Accessed June 13, 2022. https://www.lyrics.com/lyric/5212552/Don+ Moen/God+Will+Make+a+Way.

6. White, Ellen G. *Steps to Christ*. Battle Creek, MI: Review and Harold, 1898.

7. Nollen, Diana. "Cedar Rapids Sisters Say 'We Do' to 'Don't' Game Show, Showing Thursday." *The Gazette*, July 8, 2020. https://www.thegazette.com/art/cedar-rapids-say-we-do-to-dont-game-show-showing-thursday/.

8. DIY Auto Repair Videos, "Removing Scratches from Your Car Using WD-40 Hack - Final Judgement," August 29, 2015, Educational video, 4:36, https://www.youtube.com/watch?v=oKLXVNHbcvw.

9. Rollins, Walter E. "Frosty the Snowman Lyrics." Lyrics.com. Accessed May 21, 2022. https://www.lyrics.com/lyric/5065166/Gene+Autry/Frosty+the+Snowman.

10. Maxwell, Graham. *Can God Be Trusted?* Redlands, CA: Pine Knoll Publications, 2002.

11. *Hand Built Hot Rods*. Directed by Tim Vincent. Aired 2018-present, on MotorTrend.

12. *Hot Rod TV*. Season 3, episode 2, "Pure Vision." Directed by Dennis Zerull. Aired February 28, 2009, on MotorTrend.

13. Calvary Worship, Declarations, Pt. 1, *You Restore (feat. Ariel Campbell) [Live]*, Released August 23, 2019.

14. Robinson, Andrew. "Did Einstein Really Say That?" *Nature*, April 30, 2018. https://www.nature.com/articles/d41586-018-05004-4.

15. IMDb. "Toddlers & Tiaras." Accessed June 16, 2022. https://www.imdb.com/title/tt1364951/?ref_=ttfc_fc_tt.

16. Encyclopedia.com. "Wanda Holloway Trial: 1991. Accessed June 16, 2022. https://www.encyclopedia.com/law/law-magazines/wanda-holloway-trial-1991

17. Bacon, Francis. *Of Boldnesse*, published in *The Essayes or Counsels, Ciuill and Morall, of Francis Lo. Verulam, Viscount St. Alban.* London: Printed by John Haviland for Hanna Barret, 1625.

18. Greenwood, Lee. "God Bless the USA." Recorded 1984. Track B5 on *You've Got a Good Love Comin'*. Panorama Records, 1984, LP.

19. Weschler, Toni. *Taking Charge of Your Fertility: The Definitive Guide to Natural Birth Control and Pregnancy Achievement.* New York City: Harper Perennial Paperback, 1995.

20. History.com Editors. "Teen gunman kills 17, injures 17 at Parkland, Florida high school." *History*, February 6, 2019. https://www.chicagomanualofstyle.org/tools_citationguide/citation-guide-1.html.

21. *Spider-Man: No Way Home*, directed by Jon Watts (Columbia Pictures and Marvel Studios, 2021), 148 minutes.

22. *Avengers: Infinity War*, directed by Russo, Joe, and Anthony Russo (United States: Walt Disney Studios Motion Pictures, 2018), 149 minutes.

23. *Avengers: Endgame*, directed by Russo, Anthony, and Joe Russo (United States: Walt Disney Studios Motion Pictures, 2019), 182 minutes.

24. White, Ellen G. *Patriarchs and Prophets* (Washington D.C.: Re-

view and Harold Publishing Association, 1890), 34.

25. White, Ellen G. *The Story of Redemption* (Hagerstown, MD: Review and Herald Publishing Association, 1947), 28-31.

26. White, Ellen G. *The Desire of Ages*. Mountain View, CA, Portland, OR: Pacific Press Publishing Association, 1940.

27. White, Ellen G. *Christ's Object Lessons* (Washington D.C.: Review and Herald Publishing Association, 1900), 187.